color
your world
WITH PRINCESS MIRAH BATIKS

- 25 EASY PROJECTS
- SEW, KNIT OR PEEL & STICK WITH BATIKIT

C&T PUBLISHING

Text copyright © 2008 by Princess Mirah's Crafts

Artwork copyright © 2008 by C&T Publishing, Inc.

Publisher: Amy Marson

Creative Director: Gailen Runge

Acquisitions Editor: Jan Grigsby

Editor: Deb Rowden

Technical Editors: Teresa Stroin, Carolyn Aune, Sandy Peterson, Amanda Siegfried, and Nanette Zeller

Copyeditor: Stacy Chamness

Proofreader: Wordfirm Inc.

Design Director/Cover & Book Designer: Christina D. Jarumay

Production Coordinator: Kerry Graham

Illustrator: Wendy Mathson

Photography by Luke Mulks and Diane Pedersen of C&T Publishing unless otherwise noted

Published by C&T Publishing, Inc., P.O. Box 1456, Lafayette, CA 94549

Library of Congress Cataloging-in-Publication Data

Color your world with Princess Mirah Batiks : 22 easy projects, sew, knit, or peel & stick with BatiKit / Princess Mirah's Crafts.

   p. cm.

  Summary: "A book about Princess Mirah's Batiks: the woman, the history, and the fabrics. The book features home decor with a few personal items included for good measure. Princess Mirah's Crafts, fabric yarn, BatiKit, cotton and silk fabric are featured"--Provided by publisher.

  ISBN 978-1-57120-563-6 (paper trade : alk. paper)

  1. Needlework. 2. Mirah, Princess. 3. Batik--Indonesia--Bali Island. I. Princess Mirah's Crafts. II. Title.

TT751.C65 2008

746.4--dc22

                    2008002427

Printed in China

9 8 7 6 5 4 3 2 1

DEDICATION

To my grandfather the Raja.

ACKNOWLEDGMENTS

Carl Burman, Theresa Pulido, and Virginia Robertson— thank you for your valued support.

contents

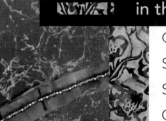

The History of Batik

The ancient art form of making batik fabrics is a time-intensive process that dates back centuries. Batik is created using wax-resist dyeing techniques. Its exact origins are unknown. Some experts believe batik originated on the island of Java. The word *batik* is Indonesian-Malay in origin and it means "to dot." Similar processes of dye-resistant designs have been traced back about 1,500 years to Egypt and the Middle East, but the current process for batik originated in Indonesia. There, batik making has evolved to become one of the greatest art forms of Asia.

Traditional batik fabric

The ancient technique involved using a *wajan*, similar in shape to a wok for melting wax, and a *canting*, a wooden-handled tool with a metal tip for applying wax to create the design. Some traditional batik designs were used exclusively by the royal courts. Over the years, trade influenced batik designs as East Indian, Dutch, and Japanese travelers began settling in Indonesia.

The Dutch brought Indonesian craftsmen to teach the craft to Dutch workers in several factories in Holland in the 1830s.

The *cap*, a traditional batik tool

For the modern-day process, a copper *cap* (chop) or stamp was created in order to improve production. This *cap* is dipped in wax and stamped on the design. Then the fabric is dyed, often numerous times, to achieve the desired effect. The fabric can also be crumpled by hand before dyeing, to achieve a textured look. The fabric is often dried outdoors, where the dyes react to the heat of the sun and become increasingly vibrant. In the final process, the wax is melted away when the fabric is immersed in a vat of hot water.

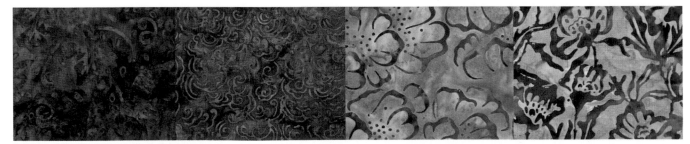

Princess Mirah's designs for Bali fabrics

Princess Mirah's Heritage

Princess Mirah is the creative force behind the beautiful batik fabrics of Bali Fabrics, Inc. She cofounded the business in Bali in 1981 to bring Balinese batiks to the North American market. Initially she worked in the fashion industry, where fashion icons used Princess Mirah batiks in their collections. Princess Mirah went on to promote the use of batiks for quilting. The trend took off and batiks became a key element for quilts of various styles.

Princess Mirah (Photo by Custom Image, Sonoma, CA)

The princess grew up in the palace of Karangasem, built by her grandfather, Anak Agung Anglurah Ketut Karangasem, the last raja in Bali.

Map of Southeast Asia—tiny Bali is highlighted in red

Princess Mirah's grandfather, the last raja

He was considered the *Raja di Raja*, or king of kings, as he had jurisdiction over eight regions in Bali even after the Dutch had annexed Indonesia. During his reign, he designed two beautiful water palaces—in the mountains, the Tirta Gangga was built around flowing spring water, while the Ujung Water Palace near the ocean was used as a place of leisure for the royal family and their guests.

One of the raja's palaces

The Karangasem palace in eastern Bali has always been Princess Mirah's home. There, age-old Hindu traditions have been kept intact, as have traditions of the Hindu Majapahit Kingdoms of Java. The palace is like a city behind walls, with medieval architecture that synthesizes elements of European, Balinese, and Chinese design. It includes a maze of pathways that open to temples and beautiful water gardens. Princess Mirah's grandfather introduced the use of water channels to Balinese architecture, so water could be piped in from springs to gardens. His living spaces created a serene yet functional setting for his family. Karangasem is like a place lost in time, where nature, art, religion, and daily life have not changed much since the raja ruled—where the village people still look to the royal family for political and spiritual direction.

Princess Mirah's grandparents in the Karangasem palace

The raja had an affinity for the artistic. He designed beautiful architectural palaces, water gardens, and temples; composed music; wrote poetry; and filled his palaces with inspirational artwork and furnishings. Princess Mirah certainly inherited her grandfather's interest in design along with the artistic skill she employs today to design new collections for Bali Fabrics.

Princess Mirah's Designs

Princess Mirah's designs for Bali Fabrics are uniquely her own and only available from Bali Fabrics. Beautiful color combinations are used to achieve truly stunning works of art. Princess Mirah's inspiration for designing is taken from traditional batiks and also her surroundings, the beautiful Balinese landscape and architecture. These design elements stand out in Princess Mirah's batik designs. Her designs often range from elegant superimposed stamps over unique layers of color to exotic color combinations reminiscent of the gardens in the royal palace. She has introduced the traditional along with the modern and cultivated the trend for using the vibrant colors and designs of batiks for quilting. She has also kept this trend alive by renewing the idea of using batiks with increasingly modern, bold designs. She created the "polos," dyed fabrics in simple color designs specifically for use in quilts. Polo is the Balinese word for background or "without pattern."

"I was so excited 26 years ago when Princess Mirah introduced her beautiful batiks to the quilt market," said designer Virginia Robertson. "The new palette of fabric has enriched my quilts. The depth of color and the rich textures of Princess Mirah's batiks have resulted in a series of 'Impressionistic' quilts. I love using these fabrics!"

In her role as co-founder and designer for Bali Fabrics, Princess Mirah's goal has always been to preserve the ancient art form of batik making and to ensure her grandfather's legacy is kept alive.

Many art quilters prefer Princess Mirah fabrics for their versatility, color, and range of design, as in *Sunrise* by Ursula Michael.

○ *Over a century ago, Claude Monet painted landscapes with random spots of paint. His technique is echoed in this quilt with the use of bits of batik fabric applied to a bright printed background. Layers of overlapping fabrics are fused to define the sunrise, allowing the picture to gradually build to a unique finish. The quilting uses different variegated threads to enhance particular areas of the landscape.*

A batik artist with Princess Mirah

Batik Designs for Home Décor

In today's do-it-yourself world, we can all function as interior designers. If you love employing color to create ambience or mood, batiks are the perfect element to help add a special touch. Princess Mirah's batiks can be found in both traditional and very modern color combinations—from subtle earth tones to intriguing tone-on-tone combinations and vibrant hues.

Surprising combinations of hues can be found in Princess Mirah's batiks. Her designs can range from rich European-influenced stamps in chartreuse coupled with lavender to rich berry florals with sap-green foliage that evoke Japanese designs to distinctly bold contemporary designs in marigold, silver, and olive tones. The vibrant designs are the most fun to use in children's and 'tweens' rooms. Bright and refreshing combinations—like one of the latest designs in red poppy and orange —are perfect for an al fresco patio setting. The luscious silk batiks in jewel tones can be used to create elegant pillows, sachets, and linings for apparel or purses.

Princess Mirah's Crafts line offers batik ribbon yarn that can be crocheted or knit into table runners, place mats, and handbags. Princess Mirah's Crafts BatiKit fabric sheets with adhesive backing are perfect for a number of crafts and for home décor. They can be used for items that range from serving trays, to lampshades, to place mats for a unique table setting.

If you're going to decorate or redesign, try something new. You might try bold hues for a summer bash, or a more exotic color design for that special dinner party you've been planning. Whatever you have in mind, using hand-dyed batiks adds a special element—much like a unique work of art that you can incorporate into your own interior designs.

MAKE ANY OR ALL OF
THESE PROJECTS TO TURN
YOUR BEDROOM INTO THE
COLORFUL RETREAT OF
YOUR DREAMS.

in the
bedroom

Concentric Squares Wallhanging

By Liz Aneloski

Size: 33½" × 33½"

Block size: 11" finished

MATERIALS

Yardage based on 42" fabric width. See Resources on page 63.

- ½ yard Princess Mirah Batik fabric 1 (floral)

- ⅝ yard Princess Mirah Batik fabric 2 (dot)

- ⅞ yard Princess Mirah Batik fabric 3 (bright)

- ⅜ yard Princess Mirah Batik fabric 4 (complementary bright) for inner border and border cornerstones

- ⅜ yard fabric for binding

- 38" × 38" backing

- 38" × 38" batting

- Basic sewing supplies

INSTRUCTIONS

Refer to your favorite basic quilting technique book for further information. Be sure to cut the selvages off the batik strips before piecing.

Cutting

Batik fabric 1 (floral)

Cut 3 strips 2½" × fabric width.

Cut 3 strips 1½" × fabric width.

Batik fabric 2 (dot)

Cut 4 strips 2½" × fabric width.

Cut 4 strips 1½" × fabric width.

Batik fabric 3 (bright)

Cut 7 strips 2½" × fabric width.

Cut 7 strips 1½" × fabric width.

Batik fabric 4 (complementary bright)

Cut 4 strips 1½" × fabric width.

Cut 4 squares 5" × 5".

Blocks

1. Cut a 2½" × 2½" square from a 2½" Batik 1 strip.

2. With right sides together, position the square on top of a 1½" Batik 3 strip, with the strip extending 2" past the top corner of the square, and aligning the side edges. Sew from approximately the center of the edge of the square to the end of the square.

Position square and sew.

3. Press the seam toward the Batik 3 and trim off the long end of the strip. *Do not trim off the 2″ extra strip tail.*

Press and trim.

4. With right sides together, position the unit from Step 3 on top of a 2½″ Batik 3 strip, as shown. Align the top and side edges, and sew.

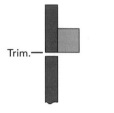

Position unit and sew.

5. Press the seam toward the Batik 3 and trim off the long end of the strip.

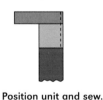

Press and trim.

6. With right sides together, position the unit from Step 5 on top of a 2½″ Batik 3 strip, as shown. Align the top and side edges, and sew.

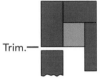

Position unit and sew.

7. Press the seam toward the Batik 3 and trim off the long end of the strip.

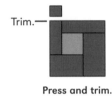

Press and trim.

8. With right sides together, position the unit from Step 7 on top of a 1½″ Batik 3 strip, as shown. Align the top and side edges. Move the beginning tail out of the way and sew.

Position unit and sew.

9. Press the seam toward the Batik 3 and trim off the strip.

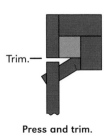

Press and trim.

10. Finish sewing the original half seam and continue sewing across the end of the Batik 3 strip.

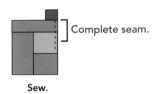

Sew.

11. Press the seam toward the Batik 3 and trim off the strip. Round 1 is complete.

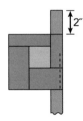

Press and trim.

12. With right sides together, position the Round 1 block from Step 11 on top of a 1½″ Batik 1 strip, aligning the long edge of the strip with the side edge of the block that contains the first narrow Batik 3 strip added in Round 1. Leave an extra 2″ of the Batik 1 strip extending past the corner of the block, as shown. Sew from approximately the center of the edge of the side to the end of the block.

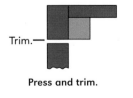

Position unit and sew.

13. Press the seam toward the Batik 3 and trim off the long end of the strip. *Do not trim off the 2″ extra strip tail.*

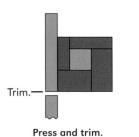

Press and trim.

14. With right sides together, position the unit from Step 13 on top of a 2½″ Batik 1 strip. Align the top and side edges, and sew.

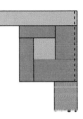

Position unit and sew.

15. Press the seam toward the Batik 3 and trim off the strip.

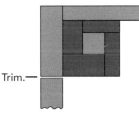

Press and trim.

16. Repeat Steps 6–11 to finish Round 2 by adding the necessary Batik 1 strips.

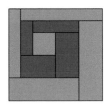

Round 2 complete

17. Repeat Steps 12–16 for Round 3 using Batik 3 strips.

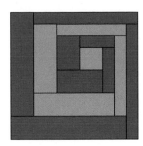

Completed block, make 2.

18. Repeat Steps 1–17 to make a second block using Batik 1 and Batik 3.

19. Repeat Steps 1–18 to make 2 blocks starting with a Batik 3 square instead of Batik 1, and using Batik 2 instead of Batik 3. Press towards the Batik 3 strips as the steps are completed.

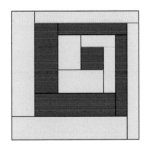

Alternate block, make 2.

20. Arrange the blocks, referring to the quilt photo (page 9) and the quilt construction illustration on page 12. Sew the blocks in pairs and then sew the pairs together.

Borders

Inner Border

1. Trim 2 strips of Batik 4 to 1½″ × 22½″. Sew to the sides of the quilt top. Press toward the inner border.

2. Trim 2 strips of Batik 4 to 1½″ × 24½″. Sew to the top and bottom of the quilt top. Press toward the inner border.

Outer Border

1. Sew 8 remaining fabric-width strips together on the long edges, alternating Batik 3 with Batik 1 or 2, and keeping the pattern of strip widths as shown in the illustration below.

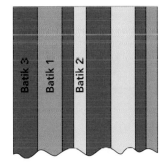

Sew border strips together.

2. Cut this strip set into 5″-wide units. You will need 8 units total.

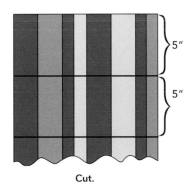

Cut.

3. Sew the 5″-wide units together in pairs, keeping the pattern of fabric placement and widths.

Sew in pairs.

4. Sew a border to each side of the quilt top. Press toward the inner border.

5. Sew a 5″ square onto each end of the remaining borders. Sew onto the top and bottom of the quilt top. Press toward the inner border.

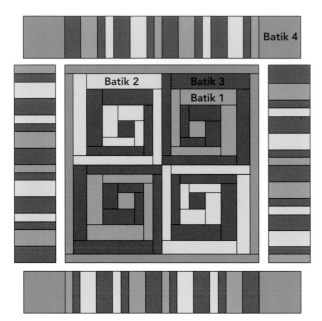

Quilt construction

Finishing

1. Layer the quilt top with batting and backing.

2. Baste, then quilt.

3. Bind using your preferred method.

Silk-Covered Lampshade

By Kerry Graham

MATERIALS

- 1 package Princess Mirah's Crafts silk chiffon fabric (21" × 36"). See Resources on page 63.
- 1 skein Princess Mirah's Crafts ½"-wide Batik rayon ribbon yarn
- Plain lampshade*
- Assorted glass beads
- Hot glue and gun
- Freezer paper
- Fabric glue
- Craft knife
- Optional: Bead reamer

*Maximum lampshade bottom diameter is approximately 12".

INSTRUCTIONS

Prepare the Ribbon

1. Fold about 5½ yards of ribbon in half lengthwise and press.

2. Fold in half lengthwise again and press.

Fold in half and press, two times.

3. You will need about 21 pieces of ribbon, each approximately 9" in length. The ribbon length depends on the size of your beads. Begin by cutting only one 9" length and follow the steps in Bead the Ribbon below. Adjust your ribbon length as needed and then cut the remaining pieces.

Bead the Ribbon

1. Ensure that the glass bead openings are wide enough to accommodate the folded ribbon. Use a bead reamer to widen the holes if necessary.

2. Twist a 9" length of ribbon through 8 beads. Tie a knot at each end of the ribbon to keep the beads on the ribbon. When attached to the shade, this will make 2 pieces of bead "fringe."

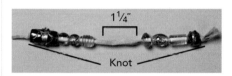

1¼"

Knot

3. Separate the beads into 2 groups of 4 beads each. There should be about 1¼" between the 2 groups of beads.

4. Repeat Steps 2 and 3 for as many bead strands as necessary. (Our lampshade needed 21 strands.)

Make the Beaded Fringe

1. You will need enough ribbon to go around the bottom edge of your lampshade plus approximately 1 yard extra for the knots. Fold and press the ribbon as in Steps 1–2 of the Prepare the Ribbon section at the left. Wind the ribbon into a ball to keep it from tangling.

2. Place a bead strand across the ribbon. Tie a knot in the ribbon around the bead strand next to one of the groups of beads.

3. Tie another knot in the ribbon around the bead strand next to the other group of beads.

4. Tie the next bead strand about 1″ away from the first.

5. Repeat Steps 2–4 for the rest of the bead strands to create a long piece of beaded fringe.

Cover the Lampshade

1. Drape the silk chiffon over the lampshade. Pin in place.

2. Remove the fabric from the lampshade and sew along the pinned line, removing each pin as you come to it.

> ### ◉ Sewing Silk Chiffon
> *Silk chiffon is a lightweight fabric. Use a sharps needle in a fine size (70/10) and a slightly shorter-than-usual stitch length.*

3. Turn the silk chiffon right side out. Pull it over the lampshade like a sleeve. Let about ½″ drape over the inside of the top of the shade. If the silk chiffon is not a tight enough fit, sew again with a slightly larger seam allowance. When you are satisfied, trim the seam allowance to ¼″ and iron the seam to one side.

4. With the silk chiffon cover centered on the lampshade, hot glue it to the inside of the top edge of the lampshade. Let any excess fabric hang down inside the shade. You will trim it later.

Glue fabric to inside edge of shade.

5. Turn the lampshade upside down and hot glue the silk chiffon to the bottom underside edge of the lampshade, the same as for the top edge in Step 4.

6. Let the glue cool, then carefully remove the excess fabric from the top and bottom edges with a craft knife. Use fabric glue to secure any loose fabric ends.

Remove excess fabric with craft knife.

Apply the Fringe

1. Apply a dot of hot glue to several knots on the beaded fringe.

2. Position the knots about ¹⁄₁₆″ up from the bottom outside edge of the lamp.

Glue fringe to shade.

3. Continue gluing the fringe in place all the way around the lamp- shade.

4. Allow the glue to cool, then let your light shine!

Silk Stripe Pillow

By Joan DeBolt
Size: 16″ × 16″

MATERIALS

- ¾ yard Princess Mirah Batik silk satin. See Resources on page 63.
- 14″ pillow form
- 1⅛ yards 22″-wide fusible interfacing
- Embroidery thread (multicolored that shows on the silk)
- Basic sewing supplies

INSTRUCTIONS

Refer to your favorite basic sewing technique book for further information.

Cutting

Piece A: 4″ × 42″, with the stripe across the short width

Piece B: 2 strips 4¼″ × 13½″, with the stripe down the length

Piece C: 2 strips 2″ × 11½″, with the stripe across the short width

Piece D: 2 strips 3″ × 16½″, with the stripe across the short width

Backing: 16½″ × 16½″

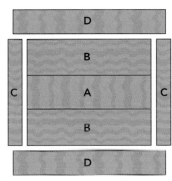

Assembly diagram

1. Sew a basting stitch down both long sides of piece A, ¼″ in from the edge. Gather evenly with the basting thread to a length of 13½″.

2. Add interfacing to the wrong side of both B strips. Using ¼″ seams, sew 1 strip to each long edge of the gathered A strip.

3. Add interfacing to the wrong side of both C strips. Sew to the short sides of the A/B unit.

4. Add interfacing to the wrong side of both D strips. Sew to the top and bottom edges. This completes the front of the pillow.

5. Add interfacing to the wrong side of the backing piece. This is the back of the pillow.

6. Sew the front to the back, right sides together, using a ¼″ seam allowance. Leave about 10″ open on one side. Turn right side out.

7. Machine stitch a feather stitch around the sewn edges ¾″ in from the edge. Use decorative embroidery thread in both the top and the bobbin.

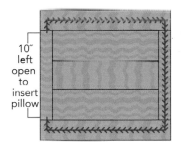

10″ left open to insert pillow

8. Insert the pillow form and press the raw edges of the opening under ¼″ to the wrong side. Hand blind-stitch closed. Carefully complete the decorative feather stitching matching the previous stitches.

9. Stitch again along the outside edge to create a second line of decorative feather stitches on all 4 sides.

Two lines of decorative stitching with multicolored thread

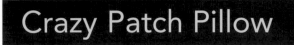

Crazy Patch Pillow

By Joan DeBolt
Size: 14˝ × 14˝

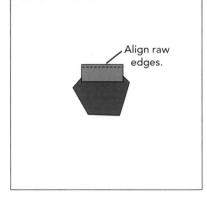

Align raw edges.

Place another piece right side down; sew.

◾◾◾ MATERIALS

- 1¼ yard Princess Mirah Batik silk satin. (Combine various amounts of Batik silk satin in different coordinating colors. Reserve a 15½˝ × 15½˝ piece for the pillow backing.) See Resources on page 63.

- 16½˝ × 16½˝ piece of lightweight fleece

- 15½˝ × 15½˝ piece of lightweight fleece

- 14˝ pillow form

- #5 perle cotton embroidery thread (in colors to go with varied silk satins)

- Clear monofilament thread

- Basic sewing supplies

◾◾◾ INSTRUCTIONS

1. Cut a piece of the darkest color silk satin in an uneven shape with 4 to 6 sides and place it right side up in the center of the 16½˝ × 16½˝ piece of fleece.

2. Place another piece of silk satin right side down on the first piece of silk satin, aligning 1 set of raw edges. Sew along these edges using a ¼˝ seam allowance. Use thread that blends with the silk satin in the top and a contrasting color in the bobbin (you will need to be able to see these bobbin lines later). Open and press. Trim.

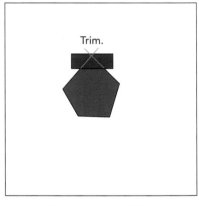

Trim.

Open, press, and trim.

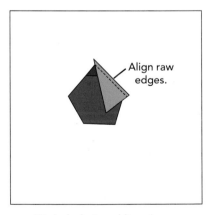

Align raw edges.

Work clockwise adding pieces.

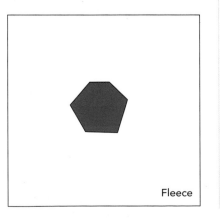

Fleece

Place silk satin right side up on fleece.

Trim.

Open, press, and trim.

3. Working in a clockwise manner, continue adding pieces of silk satin until the top is completely covered. Use pieces of various shapes so no 2 pillows will be exactly the same. Trim the pillow top to 15½˝ × 15½˝.

● For the Bobbin

The embroidery on the pillow top is bobbin work. Hand wind embroidery thread onto the bobbin and loosen the bobbin tension—this allows the thread to unwind. I recommend reserving a bobbin case especially for this. Set the stitches for the longest and widest length. Practice on a sample until you get the look you want. Consult your sewing machine manual for bobbin tension information.

4. Working with the fleece side up, select embroidery stitches on your machine. Use clear thread on the top and decorative thread in the bobbin. Follow the line of stitches on the fleece side, and stitch using various designs and colors.

5. Working on the right side of the pillow, use clear thread to add beads, buttons, braid or other embellishments. For this design, a ribbon bow was tied and stitched on flat. Strips of beaded braid were also added, as were a gold button and a wider piece of ribbon with

bobbin work down its center. When you are satisfied with your embellishments, place the pillow top wrong side down on the second piece of fleece.

6. Align the 15½˝ × 15½˝ backing right sides together with the pillow top. Stitch around all the edges using a ½˝ seam allowance. Leave an opening for the pillow form. Turn right side out. Insert the pillow form between the 2 pieces of fleece. Press the opening under ½˝ to the wrong side and stitch it closed by hand.

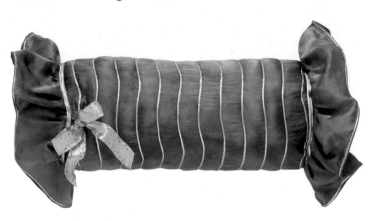

Neck Roll Pillow

By Joan DeBolt
Size: 15″ × 6″ (not including ruffles)

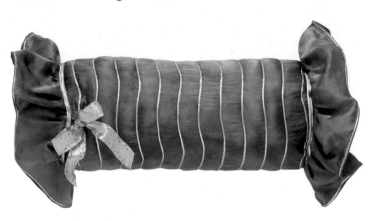

MATERIALS

- ¾ yard Princess Mirah Batik silk satin. See Resources on page 63.
- 14″ × 6″ neck roll pillow form
- 15″ × 19¾″ piece of lightweight fleece
- 8 yards ⅛″-wide gold middy braid
- 1½ yards ⅛″-wide gold bias braid
- Gold wire-edge ribbon for bow
- Clear monofilament thread
- Temporary spray adhesive
- Heavy string
- Basic sewing supplies
- *Optional: Small amount of fiberfill*

INSTRUCTIONS

1. Wrap the lightweight fleece around the pillow form and use a temporary spray adhesive to hold it in place.

2. Cut a 15″ × 19¾″ piece of silk satin for the pillow cover. Fold the fabric, short ends together, and finger crease to mark the center. Place narrow gold braid in a slightly wavy pattern along this center crease line on the right side of the fabric. Use clear thread to zigzag stitch over the braid.

3. Using the center braid as a guide, work out from the center, stitching wavy lines of braid every 1¼″ all the way to the edges.

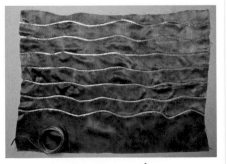

Add braid every 1¼″.

4. For the ruffles, cut 2 strips of silk satin 3½″ × 38″. Press 1 long edge and both short edges of both ruffle strips under ⅛″ to the wrong side. Repeat to create a double ⅛″ hem. Topstitch or serge the hem in place around 3 sides with matching thread.

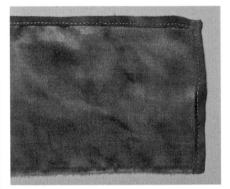

Stitch double hem on 3 sides of ruffle strips.

5. Place narrow gold braid over this hem on the right side of the fabric along the long edge. Sew the braid in place with a zigzag stitch using clear thread in the top. *Do not add braid to the hemmed short edges.*

6. Sew a basting stitch down the unfinished long edge of each ruffle, ¼″ in from the edge. Use the thread of the basting stitch to gather the unfinished edge of each ruffle to 19¾″.

7. Align each gathered ruffle edge right sides together with a long edge of the pillow cover and stitch with a ⅜″ seam allowance.

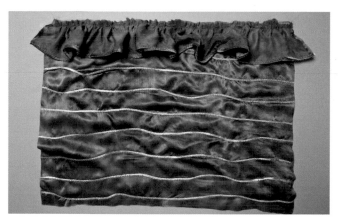

Stitch gathered ruffle to pillow cover.

8. Cut 2 pieces of silk satin 19¾″ × 5″ for the pillow ends. Press 1 long edge of each pillow end under ½″ to the wrong side; repeat to create a double ½″ hem. Topstitch the hem in place with matching thread. (Refer to the photo in Step 4 for a double hem.)

9. Align the long unfinished edge of one pillow end with the long raw edge of a ruffle, right side of the pillow end to the wrong side of the ruffle. Stitch together with a ½″ seam allowance. Repeat for the other pillow end and other ruffle.

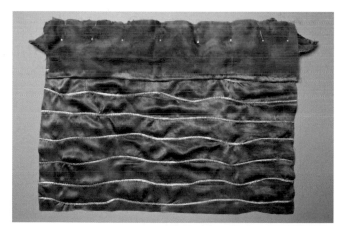

Sew pillow ends to ruffled edges.

10. Use clear thread to sew wider (middy) gold braid to the right side of the pillow cover on top of the seam where the pillow cover and the ruffle meet.

Wider gold braid covers seam.

11. Fold the pillow cover in half, right sides together, with the 2 pillow ends folded out at the ends. Fold the ruffles in, being careful not to catch them in the seam. Sew from the double hem on one pillow end to the double hem on the other pillow end with a ¼″ seam allowance. *Do not sew the double hems closed.*

Fold pillow cover in half. Do not catch ruffles or sew over double-hemmed ends.

12. Turn right side out and insert the pillow form. Add additional fiberfill to the ends if desired. Run heavy string through the double hem at each end and pull tightly. Knot the string, trim its ends, and tuck them inside the pillow.

13. Align the right sides of the hemmed short edges of the ruffles. Sew together.

14. Tie a bow with the gold wire-edge ribbon. Hand stitch the bow onto the pillow top.

🔘 **Ribbon Unravel No-More**
Run a bead of a liquid seam sealant along the ribbon ends so they don't unravel.

TREAT YOURSELF TO SOME OF
THESE LUXURIOUS THINGS—ENJOY
NOT ONLY CREATING THEM . . .
BUT USING THEM, TOO!

dressing area

Valance

By Jan Grigsby
Size: 40″–48″ window width × 17″ plus rod pocket

MATERIALS

Materials for a 40″–48″ window based on a 42″ fabric width.
Refer to Any Window You Want at right for other window widths.
See Resources on page 63.

- 1⅛ yards Princess Mirah Batik fabric 1
- 1½ yards Princess Mirah Batik fabric 2
- 1½″ curtain rod (the width of your window)
- 4 yards decorative trim
- 4 tassels
- Self-adhesive hook-and-loop tape
- Basic sewing supplies

INSTRUCTIONS

Refer to your favorite basic sewing technique book for further information.
All seam allowances are ¼″.

Cutting

From Batik 1, cut 2 strips 18″ × width of fabric (curtain).

From Batik 2, cut 2 strips 18″ × width of fabric (lining).

From Batik 2, cut 2 strips 4½″ × width of fabric (rod pocket).

○ Any Window You Want

For other window widths, measure the width of the window where you want the valance to hang. Double this measurement for the approximate fullness of the valance. Divide the fullness by 42″ (width of fabric) to get the number of strips to cut at the 18″ and 4½″ widths specified in the Cutting section.

How we calculated the cutting for our valance

Our window is 40″ wide.

40″ times 2 is 80″.

80″ divided by 42″ rounds up to 2. Therefore, we needed to cut 2 strips.

We cut 2 strips 18″ wide of each batik and 2 strips 4½″ wide of Batik 2.

Sewing

1. Sew the 18″-wide Batik 1 strips together at the short ends to make 1 long strip. Press.

2. Sew the 18″-wide Batik 2 strips together at the short ends to make 1 long strip. Press.

3. Sew the 4½″-wide Batik 2 strips together at the short ends to make 1 long strip. Press.

4. Press each short end of the 4½″-wide Batik 2 strip under ¼″ to the wrong side and stitch to create a finished edge on the 2 short ends. Press this strip in half lengthwise, right sides out.

5. Place the Batik 1 and Batik 2 strips right sides together. Stitch along 3 sides with a ¼″ seam allowance, leaving a long edge open. Turn right side out and press.

6. Align the raw edges of the narrow folded strip (rod pocket) with the raw edges of the wide strip.

7. Measure the width of the decorative trim and add ¼″ to get the trim-opening width. Place a marking pin every 17½″ across the raw edges. Double pin (2 pins together) both sides of the marking pins at a distance equal to the trim-opening width. Place other pins as necessary.

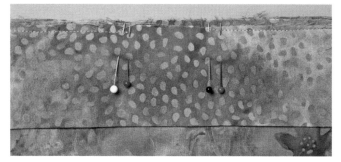

Double pins mark trim openings.

○ Tastefully Tailored

If you do not want to add trim and tassels, align the raw edges of the narrow folded strip with the raw edges of the wide strip. Pin the strips together and stitch. Press. Place the curtain rod through the rod pocket (the narrow strip) and hang as desired.

8. Begin sewing with a backstitch, then sew from the first edge to the first double pin of the first opening. Backstitch and then skip over to the next double pin, leaving the space between the pins unsewn. Backstitch and continue sewing to the next double pin. Repeat this process for all of the openings, then stitch to the end and backstitch. Press.

9. Test how much you want to draw up the valance by placing one end of the trim through an unsewn slot and pulling up from behind with the other end of the trim to get the look you want. Cut the trim that length plus approximately 2″. Place a 1″ piece of hook-and-loop tape on each end of the trim (stitch it in place to add strength). Put trim through each slot. Thread the trim through the tassel loop before hooking the trim ends together.

○ Trim Unravel No More

To prevent the decorative trim from unraveling, place a piece of tape on the trim before cutting. Cut through the tape. Leave the tape in place, use glue, or sew the trim ends so they do not unravel.

10. Place the curtain rod through the narrow strip and hang.

Vanity Stool Slipcover

By Jan Grigsby

By Jan Grigsby

MATERIALS

- 1½ yards Princess Mirah Batik fabric 1*
- 1½ yards Princess Mirah Batik fabric 2*
- Vanity stool
- Freezer paper
- Basic sewing supplies
- Optional: Trim

* Materials sufficient for a 16½″-high stool with a circular 13½″-diameter seat. Based on a 42″ fabric width, see Resources on page 63.

INSTRUCTIONS

Refer to your favorite basic sewing technique book for further information.

> **Safety First!**
> Do not make the slipcover longer than floor length, as it could be a tripping hazard.

1. Remove the stool seat or place the stool upside down on the dull, paper side of the freezer paper. Trace around the seat and add a ½″ seam allowance all around the circle. If you cannot trace the seat, measure its diameter and draw a circle with that diameter, adding a ½″ seam allowance. Cut out the freezer-paper circle.

2. Turn the stool back on its legs and measure from the seat to the floor.

3. Iron the freezer-paper circle to Batik 1 and cut out 1 circle for the seat. Remove the freezer-paper circle and iron it to Batik 2. Cut out 1 circle for the seat lining. Remove the freezer-paper circle.

> **What Kind of Paper?**
> Freezer-paper has a great use for templates in sewing. The shiny side will stick when ironed onto fabric. It can be reused several times and gently peeled away each time without leaving a trace.

4. To cut the fabric for the stool skirt, first measure around the outside of the stool seat to get its circumference. Multiply this by 1.5 to get the fullness length of fabric you will need. Divide that length by 42″ (round up) to determine the number of strips of fabric to cut.

5. To determine the width of these strips, add ¾″ (for seam allowances) to the stool height. Cut the same number of strips from both Batik 1 and Batik 2.

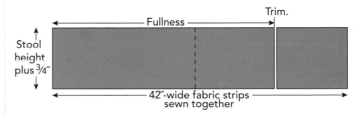

Cut enough strips to add up to fullness length.

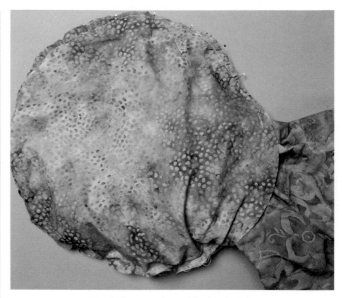

Pin circles together with skirt inside.

6. Sew the rectangles of Batik 1 together at the short ends to make a long fabric strip. Repeat for Batik 2. Trim each long fabric strip to the fullness length you calculated.

7. Align the Batik 1 and 2 long strips right sides together. Sew around 3 sides with a $\frac{1}{4}$″ seam allowance, leaving a long edge open. This is the stool skirt.

8. Turn the stool skirt right side out and press. Stitch a basting stitch along the open edge through both layers of fabric, a scant $\frac{1}{4}$″ from the edge. Evenly gather the skirt with the basting thread until the skirt fits around the seat circle, with about 1″ overlap where the ends meet.

9. Align the gathered edge of the skirt around the raw edges of the seat circle, right sides together. Pin the lining circle to the seat circle, right sides together. Keep the skirt out of the way and enclose the skirt fabric between the 2 circles. *Due to the thickness of the rectangle skirt fabric, you may not be able to pin the lining circle all the way around. Pin as much as you can.*

10. Stitch around the circle with a $\frac{1}{4}$″ seam allowance. Backstitch at the beginning and end. Leave an opening about 5″ wide for turning. Be careful not to catch more than the seam allowance of the skirt in the seam as you sew.

11. Turn by pulling the skirt fabric through the opening. Press the open edges of the circles under $\frac{1}{4}$″ to the wrong side. Pin the edges of the circles closed with $\frac{1}{4}$″ of the skirt fabric inside. Stitch the opening closed by hand with a blindstitch on both sides: the seat circle side and the lining circle side.

12. Press the slipcover. If necessary, reattach the seat back onto the legs. Place your new slipcover over the stool and have a seat!

Boudoir Box

By Susan I. Jones

MATERIALS

- 2 sheets, 12″ × 12″ each, of Princess Mirah BatiKit self-adhesive fabrics

- 18″ × 22″ piece Princess Mirah Batik silk satin in coordinating color

- Round box or jar with lid*

- Beaded fringe (length of box lid circumference)

- Tassel trim (length of box lid circumference)

- Plain, sturdy rubber band

- High-strength adhesive (see Resources, page 63)

- Spray of velvet leaves

- Decorative pin (Ours is a dragonfly.)

- Assorted glass crystals (see Resources, page 63)

- Pinking shears or decorative-edge scissors

- Craft knife

*Maximum box/jar diameter is 3¾″.

INSTRUCTIONS

1. Trace the bottom of the box onto the paper side of one of the BatiKit sheets. Cut it out.

2. With the box lid in place, measure the height of the box just up to the lid. Measure the circumference of the box. Transfer these measurements as shown onto the paper side of the other piece of BatiKit and cut it out.

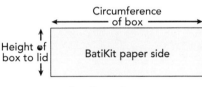

Box dimensions

3. Remove the box lid and set it aside. Remove the paper backing from the BatiKit fabric pieces and fasten them to the box.

4. Lay the silk satin piece on your work surface, wrong side up. Center the lid on the fabric with the inside of the lid down.

5. Apply glue around the side of the lid. Gather the silk satin fabric in one hand over the glued edge, evenly distributing the fabric around the lid. Secure the fabric with a rubber band in the center of the top of the lid.

Rubber band secures fabric.

6. When the glue is dry, use pinking shears or other edging scissors and trim away the excess fabric in the center of the lid top. Trim the fabric to about ¼″ from the lid edges, leaving a nice flounce.

Trim excess fabric.

7. Remove the fabric from the inside of the lid, trimming the fabric along the glued edge with a craft knife.

Trim along inside edge.

8. Put the lid on the box. Glue the beaded fringe around the lid edge. Glue the tassel fringe on top of the beaded fringe around the lid edge.

9. Arrange the flounce on the box lid and glue the velvet leaf spray in place. Glue the decorative pin onto the leaf spray.

10. Further embellish the lid and the trims with tiny crystals.

Wild Fiber Necklace

By Susan I. Jones

Size: 20″–22″ long necklace

MATERIALS

- 1 skein Princess Mirah's Crafts Marigold ¼″ Batik cotton ribbon yarn

- 1 skein Princess Mirah's Crafts Garnet ½″ Batik cotton ribbon yarn

- 1 skein Princess Mirah's Crafts Wild Lime ¼″ Batik cotton ribbon yarn

- 1 skein fine eyelash yarn (see Resources, page 63)

- Crochet hook, size Q (16mm)

- Large-eye embroidery needle

- Assortment of 16–24 lightweight beads (small, medium, and large diameters)

- Assortment of 18–30 large-hole spacer beads (gold, silver, or copper)

- 1–3 large pendant bead(s) (to hang at the base of the necklace as the focal point)

- Large jump ring(s) or beading wire

- Beading pliers

- Jewelry glue

INSTRUCTIONS

Refer to your favorite basic crochet technique book for further information.

1. String 8–14 beads onto the eyelash yarn using a large-eyed embroidery needle. Do not cut the yarn.

2. Leave a beginning 10″ tail and crochet a single chain with the Garnet ribbon yarn and the eyelash yarn held together. While chain stitching, push up the beads randomly in the stitches to distribute them every 1½″–3″ along the chain. Make the chain 20″–22″ long. Knot off and cut the 2 yarns, leaving a 10″ ending tail.

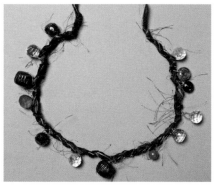

Randomly distribute beads in chain.

3. Repeat Steps 1 and 2 with the Marigold ribbon yarn and the eyelash yarn.

4. String 8–14 large-hole spacer beads onto the Wild Lime ribbon yarn, using the embroidery needle if necessary. Repeat Step 2 with only the Wild Lime ribbon yarn.

5. Evenly and tightly twist the 3 beaded chains together and knot securely at both ends to retain the twist.

6. String 8–14 spacer beads onto the Marigold ribbon yarn. Repeat Step 2 with the Marigold ribbon yarn and the Wild Lime ribbon yarn.

7. Leaving a 10″ beginning and ending tail, single chainstitch a 20″–22″ length with the Garnet ribbon yarn.

8. Twist all 5 ribbon chains loosely together and knot together securely at both ends.

9. Determine the center point of the necklace. Attach the focal bead(s) at this point with the jump ring(s) or beading wire through a chainstitch and secure.

10. Slip all the strands of 1 tail of the necklace through a spacer bead. Slide the spacer bead up next to the knot and secure with a dab of glue. Repeat on the other tail end.

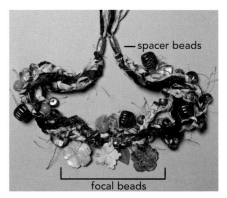

— spacer beads

focal beads

Add spacer beads to tails.

11. To wear the necklace, tie the ends into a loose bow.

Clutch Bag

By Susan I. Jones
Size: 12" × 5½"

Attach magnet to fleece and fabric.

MATERIALS

- 12" × 16½" Princess Mirah Batik fabric 1 for outside

- 12" × 16½" Princess Mirah Batik fabric 2 for lining

- 2 pieces, 2" × 9¼" each, Princess Mirah Batik fabric 2 for binding

- 1 skein Princess Mirah's Crafts ½"-wide Batik rayon ribbon yarn (to match Batik fabric 1)

- 11⅞" × 16⅜" fleece

- Size 13 (9mm) knitting needles

- Large decorative button, antique brooch, or other embellishment

- Magnetic snap for handbags

- Decorative thread to coordinate with Batik fabric 1

- Fabric glue

- Basic sewing supplies

- *Optional: Sequined yarn*

INSTRUCTIONS

Refer to your favorite basic knitting technique book for further information. The following abbreviations are used in this project:

CO = cast on

ST = stitches

BO = bind off

1. Knitted piece: Holding the ribbon yarn and optional sequined yarn together, CO 10 ST. Knit every row until this piece measures approximately 4½" × 12". BO loosely. Set aside. (See above for a key to the abbreviations.)

2. Layer the Batik 1 fabric and the fleece, with the wrong side of the batik toward the fleece. Attach the female part of the magnetic snap to the batik and the fleece with the wrong side of the snap down on the right side of the batik. Place the center of the snap 1¼" from a raw edge and 6¼" from either side.

○ **Snap To It**

To attach the magnetic snap, first determine its correct position. Then make 2 small (⅛" long) slits in the fabric and fleece for the 2 snap prongs. Push the prongs through the fabric and fleece. Place the snap back guard over the prongs on the fleece side. Bend the prongs over the back guard to secure the snap in place.

Prongs bent over snap back guard

3. Layer the Batik 2 fabric with the Batik 1 fabric and the fleece, right sides together with the Batik 1 fabric. Stitch the 3 layers together with a ¼" seam allowance across the top and bottom (the short sides). Turn the unit right side out and press. The fleece should be sandwiched between the 2 batiks.

4. Topstitch across each sewn edge, ⅛" in from the edge. Use a decorative thread.

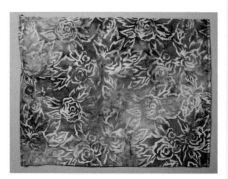

Topstitch top and bottom of clutch unit.

5. Place the clutch unit, Batik 1 fabric side up. Fold the end with the magnet over 4"; this is the bottom edge of the clutch. Fold the other end over 3"; this is the top edge of the clutch.

Fold clutch unit, outside fabric sides together.

6. Fold and press 1 short end of each Batik 2 fabric binding piece ¼" to the wrong side. Then fold and press each binding piece in half lengthwise, wrong sides together.

7. Align the raw edges of a binding piece with the raw edges on 1 side of the clutch unit. Pin in place. The ¼" folded edge of the binding piece should align with the bottom edge of the clutch. Repeat for the other binding piece on the other raw side edges of the clutch.

Pin and stitch binding to clutch unit.

8. Stitch together the binding and the clutch unit with a ¼" seam allowance.

9. Fold the binding over the seam allowance to the other side of the clutch and hand blindstitch it to the Batik 2 fabric (the lining of the clutch).

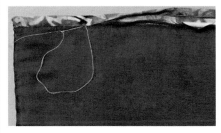

Blindstitch binding to lining.

10. Turn the clutch unit right side out and hand blindstitch the top of the clutch unit (the side without a magnet, at this point) to the lining.

Blind stitch top of clutch to lining.

11. Place the clutch with the lining showing and the magnet at the bottom. Fold the top of the unit down 3¾" to form the clutch flap. Determine the position of the remaining (male) magnetic snap component on the center of the flap. Snip holes carefully through all the layers and attach the snap. Refer to Snap To It on page 27 for more instruction. (The knitted piece will cover the hardware on the front of the flap.)

Front view   **Back view**

Attach snap.

12. Position the knitted piece in the center of the outside of the clutch, aligning a short edge of the knitting with the top edge of the clutch front flap, matching edges. Wrap the knitted piece around the bottom of the clutch and around the female portion of the snap. Pin, then glue in place.

13. Glue or stitch the decorative button or other embellishment to the center of the front of the clutch, over the knitted piece and the snap hardware.

Lavender/Cedar Sachet

By Mari Dreyer
Size: approximately 3"

▨ MATERIALS

Makes 1 sachet. See Resources on page 63.

- 16" × 16" Princess Mirah's Crafts silk chiffon fabric
- 19" × 19" tulle in coordinating color
- ¾ cup dried lavender (or other sachet filler)
- ¼ cup fine cedar shavings (available at bed and bath shops)
- Satin cording in coordinating color
- Vintage or other large button

▨ INSTRUCTIONS

1. Cut 1 circle approximately 14" in diameter from the silk chiffon.

2. Cut 1 circle approximately 18" in diameter from the tulle.

3. Center the silk chiffon on the tulle.

4. Mix together the dried lavender and the cedar shavings (or other sachet filler) and pour the lavender/cedar mix in a mound onto the center of circle.

5. Carefully gather the silk chiffon and tulle, arranging the fabric until it's ready to tie closed.

6. Tie a secure double knot with the cording, then thread the ends of the cording through the button.

7. Tie a bow over the button with the cording.

8. Trim the cording ends and knot. Apply a drop of glue to the knot to keep it from unraveling.

Batik Silk Satin Eye Pillow

By Mari Dreyer
Size: 8½" × 4"

▨ MATERIALS

- 2 pieces, 9" × 4½" each, Princess Mirah's Batik silk satin. See Resources on page 63.
- 1 piece, 9" × 4½", tulle in a coordinating color
- Decorative glass beads (for corners)
- Pretreated photo fabric sheet (large enough to print a photo 6¼" × 1¾")
- Sachet filler mixture (or purchase a mixture of your choice):
  - ½ cup dried lavender
  - ½ cup whole flaxseed

▨ INSTRUCTIONS

1. Place the 2 rectangles, 9" × 4½", of silk satin right sides together.

2. Sandwich the tulle between the 2 silk satin rectangles, pin, and sew 3 sides together with a ¼" seam allowance, leaving a short end open. Turn right side out.

3. Using your favorite photo software program, crop a photo to 6¼" wide × 1¾" high (adjust this to your personal preference).

4. Print the photo onto the photo fabric sheet following the manufacturer's instructions and cut it out.

5. Insert the photo between the tulle and the silk satin.

6. Fill the pillow with the lavender/flaxseed mix and hand stitch the opening closed.

7. Embellish the corners with beads as in the photo.

> **O Right or Wrong?**
> *Princess Mirah's Crafts Batik cotton, silk satin, and silk chiffon fabrics do not have a "right" or "wrong" side. Both sides are equally beautiful. When we refer to a "right side," it is to allow you to pick your favorite side knowing that will be the side that shows once the project is completed.*

YOU DON'T HAVE TO BE
A 'TWEEN TO HAVE FUN
WITH THESE CREATIONS—
THEY ARE OH-SO-RIGHT
FOR ANYONE WHO'S
YOUNG AT HEART.

fun colors
for 'tweens

Windy Path Throw

By Liz Aneloski

Size: 46½″ × 52½″

Block size: 6″ finished

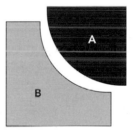 **INSTRUCTIONS**

Refer to your favorite basic quilting technique book for more information. This is a traditional Drunkard's Path block.

Blocks

1. Cut a random assortment of 42 pieces using template A and 42 using template B from the 8 block batiks.

2. Choose an A piece and a B piece that make a block. Group 42 pairs of A and B pieces.

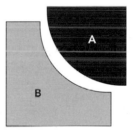

Group 42 pairs.

3. Arrange the A/B pieces into 7 rows of 6 blocks. Rearrange the batik pairs until you are satisfied with the design.

4. Fingerpress the seam allowance under on each curved edge. Unfold. (This makes it easier to align the 2 curved edges.)

5. Place the A/B pieces right sides together, and place pins in the center, at both ends, and in several places along the curved edge.

Pin.

MATERIALS

Yardage is based on 42″ fabric width. See Resources on page 63.

- ⅜ yard each 8 Princess Mirah Batik fabrics for blocks

- ¼ yard Princess Mirah Batik 1 fabric for inner border*

- ¾ yard Princess Mirah Batik 2 fabric for outer border*

- ⅝ yard Princess Mirah Batik 3 fabric for binding*

- 51″ × 57″ backing

- 51″ × 57″ batting

- Basic sewing supplies

  * *Choose your favorite 3 batiks from the 8 block batiks.*

6. Sew along the curved edge, smoothing the layer as you go, to prevent any tucks in the seam.

> **O Have It Your Way**
> *Some quilters prefer to stitch with piece A on top; some quilters prefer to stitch with B on top. Try both ways to see which you prefer.*

7. Press toward piece B. Make 42 blocks.

Make 42.

Quilt Construction

1. Sew the blocks into rows. Press, alternating the pressing direction of the seams: Row 1 to the right, Row 2 to the left, and so on.

2. Sew the rows together. Press the seams in one direction.

Inner Border

1. Measure the quilt top through the center from top to bottom. If this measurement is equal to or shorter than your usable fabric width (fabric width with selvages removed), cut 2 strips 1½″ × fabric width and remove the selvages. If this measurement is longer than your usable fabric width, cut 3 strips, remove the selvages, and sew them into one long length. Cut 2 strips to the top-to-bottom measurement.

2. Sew a strip to each side of the quilt and press toward the inner border.

3. Measure the quilt top through the center from side to side. Cut 2 strips 1½″ × fabric width and remove the selvages. Cut these 2 strips to the side-to-side measurement.

4. Sew strips to the top and bottom edges of the quilt top and press toward the inner border.

Outer Border

1. Measure the quilt top through the center from side to side. Cut 2 strips 4½″ × fabric width and remove the selvages. Cut these 2 strips to this side-to-side measurement.

2. Sew strips to the top and bottom edges of the quilt top and press toward the inner border.

3. Measure the quilt top through the center from top to bottom. Cut 3 strips 4½″ × fabric width, remove the selvages, and sew them into one long length. Cut 2 strips to the top-to-bottom measurement.

4. Sew a strip to each side edge of the quilt top and press toward the inner border.

Finishing

1. Layer the quilt top with batting and backing.

2. Baste, then quilt.

3. Bind using your preferred method.

Quilt construction

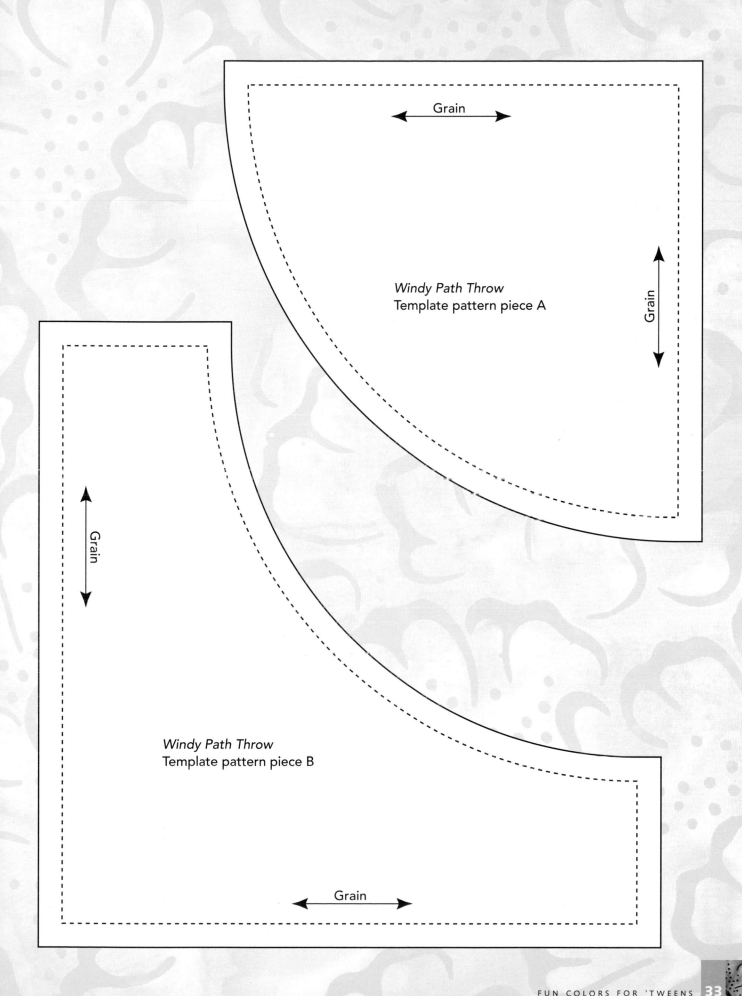

Grain

Windy Path Throw
Template pattern piece A

Grain

Grain

Windy Path Throw
Template pattern piece B

Grain

Altered Game Board

By Kristi Van Doren

MATERIALS

For additional product information, see Resources on page 63.

- Wooden or plastic game set (Our set had checkers on one side and tic-tac-toe on the other.)

- 3 sheets, 12″ × 12″ each, Princess Mirah's Crafts BatiKit self-adhesive fabric in coordinating patterns/colors

- Glitter in 2 complementary colors

- ⅛″-and ⅜″-wide double-stick tape

- Hot glue gun and glue

- High-strength adhesive

- Clear-drying craft glue

- Nonstick craft sheet

- Rubber stamps

- Variegated gold leafing

- Craft heating tool

- Stiff stencil brush

- Craft blade

INSTRUCTIONS

1. Measure the individual game squares. Cut the BatiKit to size and apply the squares to the game board, alternating the colors to match the layout of the game board.

2. Measure, cut, and apply BatiKit border strips.

3. Use a fine-point tip and apply clear-drying craft glue to all the squares' edges. Sprinkle with the desired color of glitter. (We used lime green on our checkerboard.)

4. Apply glue around the perimeter of the top of the board and add glitter in another color. (We used purple.) Set the top aside to dry.

5. Cut a 1″ strip of BatiKit and attach it to all sides of the game board base. Decorate it with ⅛″ double-stick tape and apply glitter.

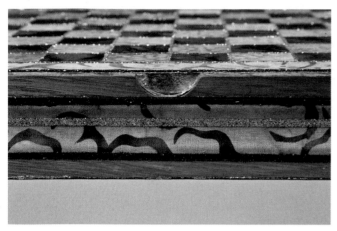

Embellish sides of game board base.

6. Place ⅜″ tape around the top edge of the game board base and apply variegated leafing. Brush off the excess and set aside.

Variegated leafing embellishment

7. Using a hot glue gun, squeeze some glue onto a nonstick craft sheet. Push the stamp of your choice into the glue and let it cool completely. Remove the stamp and apply a small amount of heat with a heat tool until the surface of the glue is glossy but the design is still visible. Apply leafing to the glue and gently tap the leafing into the design. Brush away the excess leafing with a stiff stencil brush.

8. Cut the glue embellishments in half with a craft blade. Align the straight edges with the edges of the game board top and glue in place with high-strength adhesive.

Apply glue embellishments that are cut in half.

9. Turn the game board top over and decorate the back following Steps 1–5 above. Let it dry.

10. When the top of the game board is completely dry, apply ⅜″ double-sided tape to the side edge of the top and add variegated leafing.

11. Place the game pieces on the paper side of a sheet of BatiKit and trace the dimension of the circles. Cut out the circles and attach them to both sides of the game pieces, varying the colors of BatiKit to match the game pieces.

12. Apply a small amount of glue or double-sided tape to the sides of the game pieces and add glitter. Set aside on a nonstick craft sheet to dry.

Apply BatiKit and glitter to game pieces.

13. Set up the game board to play and enjoy!

Crocheted Round Rugs in Three Sizes

By Veline Ball

Diameter sizes: 20″, 22½″, and 27″

**MATERIALS**

■ Size N (10mm) aluminum crochet hook

Note: Using an aluminum hook is best because the flannel strips will stick to crochet hooks made from other materials.

Small Rug

■ 20 skeins of Princess Mirah's Crafts cotton flannel ½″ ribbon yarn (We used Sunny Lime.) See Resources on page 63.

Medium Rug

■ 22 skeins of Princess Mirah's Crafts cotton flannel ½″ ribbon yarn (We used Razzmatazz Red.)

Large Rug

■ 31 skeins of Princess Mirah's Crafts cotton flannel ½″ ribbon yarn (We used Dusty Lavender.)

■ 6 skeins of Princess Mirah's Crafts cotton flannel ½″ ribbon yarn for scallop edging (We used Razzmatazz Red.)

**INSTRUCTIONS**

Refer to your favorite basic crocheting technique book for further information.

The following abbreviations are used in this project:

ch = chain

sl st = slip stitch

dc = double crochet

tr = treble crochet

sc = single crochet

Small Rug

Leaving a beginning 1½″ tail, ch 4.

Insert hook into first ch and sl st to form a circle. Ch 2.

Round 1

11 dc into center of the ring, making sure to catch the tail to cover it as you go.

Sl st in top of starting ch to join. Ch 2.

Round 2

Working in **back loops only** throughout the rest of the project, dc in same space as starting ch.

*2 dc in each of next 2 dc, 3 dc in next dc. Repeat from * around.

Sl st in top of starting ch to join. Ch 2.

Round 3

1 dc in same stitch as starting ch.

2 dc in each of next 2 dc, 1 dc in next dc.

*2 dc in each of next 3 dc, 1 dc in next dc. Repeat from * around.

Skip last and join with sl st in top of starting ch. Ch 2.

Round 4

1 dc in same stitch as starting ch. *1 dc in each of next 5 dc, 2 dc in next dc. Repeat from * around.

Join with sl st in top of starting ch. Ch 2.

Round 5

1 dc in same stitch as starting ch.

*2 dc in next dc, 1 dc in top of next 2 dc. Repeat from * around.

Join with sl st in top of starting ch. Ch 2.

Round 6

1 dc in each next 40 dc, 2 dc in next dc, 1 dc in each dc to the end of round.

Join with sl st in top of starting ch. Ch 2.

Round 7

1 dc in each of next 12 dc, 2 dc in next dc.

*1 dc in each of next 13 dc, 2 dc in next dc. Repeat from * around to last 9 dc.

1 dc in each of next 9 dc.

Join with sl st in top of starting ch. Ch 2.

Round 8

1 dc in same stitch as starting ch, 1 dc in each of next 7 dc.

*2 dc in next dc, 1 dc in each of next 7 dc. Repeat from * around until last 4 dc.

1 dc in each of next 4 dc.

Join with sl st in top of starting ch. Ch 2.

Round 9

1 dc in each of next 2 dc.

*2 dc in next dc, 1 dc in each of next 3 dc. Repeat from * around to last 2 dc.

2 dc in next dc, 1 dc in each of next dc.

Join with sl st in top of starting ch. Ch 2.

Round 10

1 dc in same stitch as starting ch.

*1 dc in each of next 7 dc, 2 dc in next dc. Repeat from * around until last 7 dc.

1 dc in each of next 7 dc.

Join with sl st in top of starting ch. Ch 2.

Round 11

Repeat Round 10 to last 6 dc. End round with 1 dc in each of next 5 dc, 2 dc in each of next dc.

Join with sl st in top of starting ch.

Tie off and block rug (see tip on page 38).

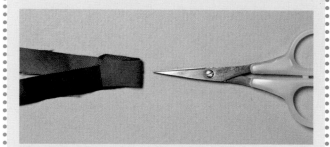

Medium Rug

Work Rounds 1–11, same as small rug, ending row 11 with ch 2 after joining.

Round 12

1 dc in each of next 7 dc.

*2 dc in next dc, dc in each of next 8 dc. Repeat from * around to last 1 dc.

2 dc in last dc.

Join with sl st in top of starting ch.

Tie off and block rug.

Large Rug with Scalloped Edge

Work rounds 1 through 12, same as for medium rug, with ch 2 after joining.

Round 13

1 dc in same stitch as starting ch.

*1 dc in each of next 9 dc, 2 dc in next dc. Repeat from * around.

Join with sl st in top of starting ch. Ch 2.

Round 14

1 dc in same stitch as starting ch.

*1 dc in each of next 14 dc, 2 dc in next dc. Repeat from * around to last 6 dc.

1 dc in each of next 6 dc.

Change color by pulling through new color when joining with a sl st (leave a 3" tail to tie off with new color, then trim and weave in end).

Ch 2 with edging color.

Round 15 (Scalloped Edging Round)

Still working in back loops: 1 sc in next dc.

*1 dc in next dc, 2 tr in next dc, 1 dc in next dc, 1 sc in each of next 2 dc. Repeat from * around to last 4 dc.

1 dc in next dc, 2 tr in next dc, 1 dc in next dc, 1 sc in next dc.

Join with a sl st in top of starting ch.

Tie off and block rug.

Coil Pots

By Maria Allison

Sizes: 5″ × 2½″ diameter (tall round pot),
3″ × 3″ × 5½″ (oval pot),
2½″ × 5″ diameter (square pot)

MATERIALS

- 1 skein Princess Mirah's Crafts cotton flannel ½″-wide ribbon yarn for each pot. See Resources on page 63.

- Approximately 6 yards of cotton clothesline or ¼″ upholstery cording for each pot

- Fabric glue

- Optional: Fabric flowers, ribbon, glitter, beads

INSTRUCTIONS

It is best to wrap the clothesline needed for each project before starting to shape it into a pot. Securing the end with the glue, wrap the ribbon yarn around the clothesline. Glue the ribbon yarn to the clothesline every 4″–5″ to keep the ribbon yarn in place.

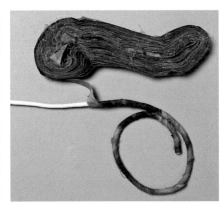

Wrap ribbon yarn around clothesline.

Make the Tall Round Pot

1. To make the base of the pot, coil one end of the wrapped clothesline into a disk, gluing the coils together as you go.

Circular pot base

2. When the base is approximately 3″ in diameter, start to build the sides by coiling the covered clothesline on top of it. The sides will be straight if the clothesline coils are directly on top of each other. The sides will widen if the coils are glued on each previous coil's outside edge.

Coils are glued to outer edge of previous coils.

3. Finish by wrapping the end of the ribbon yarn around the end of the clothesline so it cannot be seen. Glue the very end of the fabric to the inside of the pot.

Make Pots in Other Shapes

For oval pots: Instead of coiling the beginning of the clothesline into a tight circle, start by folding the clothesline 1″–2″ from the end. Continue coiling the clothesline around this folded end until the base is 2″ × 4¼″, then build up the sides.

Oval pot base

For square pots: Begin with a circle base. When it is 2½″ in diameter, fold the clothesline into right angles to make corners and tack it to the coil base. Glue ribbon yarn in the spaces between the corners and the circle base to cover the gaps. Build up the sides, making sure the corners do not become too rounded.

Square pot base

For larger pots: Wrap ribbon yarn strips around a *longer* piece of clothesline. Coil the bottom to the desired size and build up the sides to the desired height. When adding new strips of ribbon yarn, just overlap the added strip over the previous strip and glue in place. If you must add a new piece of clothesline before your pot is finished, butt the ends of the line together, secure with hand stitching, and continue to cover with the strips.

Floral Canvas Collage

By Becky Chabot
*Sizes: 12″ × 12″, 12″ × 36″,
and 12″ × 12″*

MATERIALS

- 4 sheets, 12″ × 12″ each, Princess Mirah's Crafts BatiKit fabric with adhesive backing (4 patterns)

- 1 skein Princess Mirah's Crafts ½″-wide cotton ribbon yarn [Wild Lime]

- 3 traditional stretched canvases: 1 canvas 12″ × 36″ and 2 canvases 12″ × 12″

- Denim colorwash spray

- Gold webbing spray

- Workable fixative spray

- ½″-wide double-sided tape

- Kelly green seed beads

- Sewing needle and thread

INSTRUCTIONS

1. Completely cover the canvas pieces with the denim colorwash spray. Spritz with water.

2. Crumple 3–4 paper towels and dab excess moisture randomly to create texture and tone. Let dry.

3. Spray the canvases with gold webbing. Let dry, then spray with workable fixative or other sealant. (Color washes are water based and should be sealed.)

4. Cut the 4 pieces of 12″ × 12″ BatiKit in half diagonally to create half-square triangles and create a background pattern as shown. Starting on the long right-hand side, place the first triangle near the top along the right edge of the largest canvas, peel, and stick. Place the second triangle near the bottom along the right edge. Place a third triangle on the left side of the large canvas, centered in relation to the triangles on the right. Cut 1 half-square triangle in half to create 2 quarter-square triangles. Place a quarter-square triangle in the top left corner and the other in the bottom left corner.

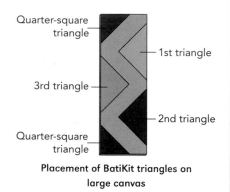

Placement of BatiKit triangles on large canvas

5. Place a 12″ × 12″ canvas on either side of the large canvas. Continue placing the half-square triangles of BatiKit as if they were full squares of fabric running over onto the next canvas. Slightly offset some of them for added interest. Trim the BatiKit to the front edge of the canvas.

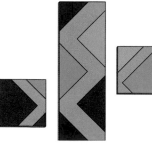

Placement of BatiKit triangles on small canvases

6. Place strips of double-sided tape on the canvas and accordion-fold the green ribbon yarn onto the adhesive to create "stems." Trim at the edge of the canvas.

Fold green ribbon to create stems.

7. String beads, sew the beads in a row on top of the stems, and then anchor the thread through the canvas. (Refer to the project photos on page 41.)

8. Trim the stems on the back of the flower heads flush so they lie flat on the canvas. Sew or glue the flowers to the canvas.

9. Rub the edges of the canvas randomly with glitter glue and spread it toward the center of the canvas.

Pocket Book

By Lisa Fulmer Bruce
Size: 5″ × 7″

▰▰▱▰ MATERIALS

- 7″ × 5″ Ready to Go! Blank Board Book. See Resources on page 63.

- 2 pieces 7½″ × 14″ Princess Mirah's Crafts Batik fabric

- 10 pieces 5″ × 6⅞″ Princess Mirah's Crafts BatiKit fabric with adhesive backing (for pages)

- 1 piece 4½″ × 5¼″ Mirah Crafts BatiKit fabric with adhesive backing (for spine)

- 5 pieces 3⅞″ × 4⅞″ Quilter's Vinyl (for inside pocket pages)

- 4″ × 6″ cardstock (for inside front cover)

- Rickrack and/or thin ribbon

- Seed beads, small beads, and charms

- 2 metal tag holders

- 4 jewel brads

- Assorted adhesive acrylic dots (2 should match the size of the metal tag holders)

- Double-sided tape

- Scissors

- 2 colors of embroidery floss

- Beading needle

- Embroidery needle

- Wide-tip permanent marker (in a complementary color)

- Dark fine-point permanent marker

- Pinhole punch or awl

- Small, thin glue dots

- High-strength adhesive

- Ruler

- Craft blade

- Small self-healing cutting mat

INSTRUCTIONS

Cover the Blank Board Book

1. Color the edges and a ¼″ border around all the pages with the wide-tip marker.

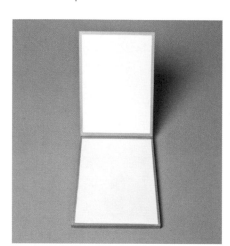

Color edges and borders.

2. Press 1 short edge of a 7½″ × 14″ piece of batik fabric under ¼″ to the wrong side.

3. Open the book to the inside cover page. Center the pressed fabric edge on the short side of the book and adhere it to the inside cover, ¹⁄₁₆″ away from the spine, with double-sided tape.

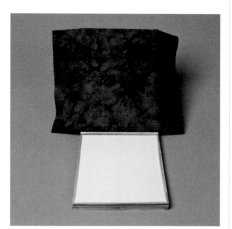

Adhere fabric to inside cover.

4. Fold the fabric in half over the length of the cover. Press the fold. Position the fabric on the outside cover ¼″ from the spine. Tape in place with double-sided tape.

Tape fabric to front cover.

5. Trim the inside flaps flush with the sides of the inside cover, and secure the flaps to the inside cover with double-sided tape.

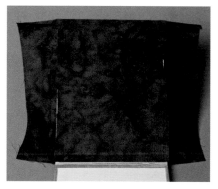

Trim and tape inside flaps.

6. Trim the outside flap to 1″. Fold and miter all 4 corners of the outside flap like wrapping a gift. Wrap tightly and smoothly to the inside; turn the edge under ¼″. Secure the fabric to the inside of the book from underneath with double-sided tape.

7. Repeat Steps 1–6 on the back cover of the book using the other 7½″ × 14″ piece of batik fabric.

Miter corners.

8. Adhere a 5″ × 6⅞″ piece of a BatiKit to each book page. End approximately ⅛″ from the book spine.

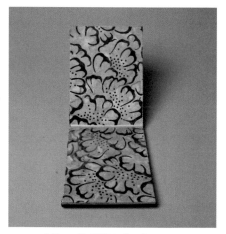

Adhere BatiKit to book pages.

9. If necessary, trim away excess BatiKit with a craft blade on a cutting mat. If any white shows around the edges of the BatiKit, color it in with the wide-tip marker.

Cover the Spine

1. Place a 4½″ × 5¼″ piece of BatiKit on the table, lining side up. Center the book spine on the sheet so about 2″ of the BatiKit will wrap onto the front and back covers evenly.

2. Mark both sides of the spine on the lining and cut notches so the paper is flush with the 5″ edge. The BatiKit will wrap ⅛″ around the edges of the 7″ sides over the fabric.

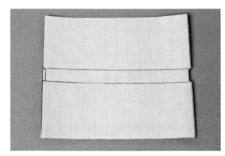

Mark and cut notches.

3. Peel away the liner, center, and position the BatiKit on the spine first, then smooth onto the front and back covers.

Front Cover Embellishments

1. Use a fine-point marker and ruler to mark pinhole-size dots ⅜″ in from each side on the front cover. Start ½″ from the bottom, space them ½″ apart, and end about 1″ from the spine.

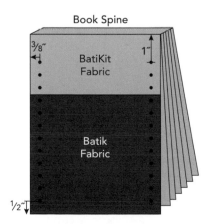

Punch dots on front cover.

2. Use the awl or pinpoint punch to punch a small hole at each mark.

3. Cut a 25″ length of 6-strand embroidery floss and thread it through the beading needle.

4. Starting inside the front cover at one of the holes closest to the spine, point the needle through the hole to the outside. Add 1–2 small beads and a charm, then bring the needle all the way out and down through the next hole. Leave an 8″–9″ beginning tail of embroidery floss inside the front cover.

5. Continue stitching and adding beads until you get to the last hole at the outer edge. Leave an 8″–9″ length of floss at this end, also. Pull the floss to tighten the stitches as needed.

6. Repeat for the other side of the front cover, again leaving 8″–9″ tails at the beginning and end. Bring the floss ends across the 5″ side and tie into bows at opposite diagonal corners to create a frame. Trim the ends of the bows and seal with a dab of glue.

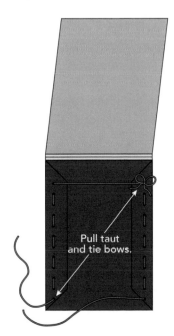

Tie bows inside front cover; seal with glue.

Back Cover Thread Grid

1. Repeat Steps 1–3 in Front Cover Embellishments (above) for the back cover.

2. Starting inside the back cover at one of the holes closest to the spine, point the needle through the hole to the outside. Add 1–2 small beads, then bring the needle all the way out and back down in the hole directly across from the first hole on the other side. Leave an 8″–9″ beginning tail of embroidery floss inside the back cover.

3. Point the needle through the hole directly under the first hole, creating a diagonal stitch across the inside of the back cover. Repeat this stitch until you reach the outer edge, creating a grid to tuck things inside. Leave an 8″–9″ ending tail at this end, also. Pull the floss to tighten the stitches as needed.

4. Bring the floss ends across the book, loop around the floss at the other side, and knot. Trim the ends and seal with a dab of glue.

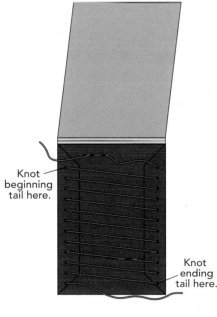

Knot floss ends inside back cover; seal with glue.

Make Pockets

1. With a fine-point marker and ruler, mark 8 holes ½˝ apart and ¼˝ in from each side of pages 1, 3, 5, 7, and 9. The first hole is ⅛˝ up from the bottom. The last holes are 3⅜˝ in from the spine. Mark 10 holes across the bottom, also at ½˝ intervals. Punch the holes.

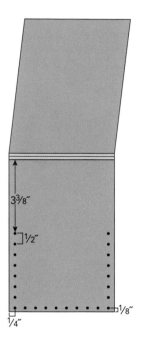

Punch holes on odd-numbered pages.

2. Place a small glue dot at each corner of the Quilter's Vinyl. Adhere it to the page, aligned evenly with the bottom and allowing a slight buckle from side to side so the pocket is not too tight across the width of the page.

3. Thread 6 strands of embroidery floss through an embroidery needle, and knot at the end. Starting at one of the holes in the center of the page, point the needle down to go through the vinyl and the hole. Pull the needle all the way through, then come back up through the next hole. Continue stitching all the way around through the book page and the vinyl, ending back at the top of the pocket. Pull the stitches taut and knot the floss ends. Trim the ends as close as possible to the knots. Place small adhesive acrylic dots over the knots.

4. Repeat Steps 2–3 for the remaining 4 pages.

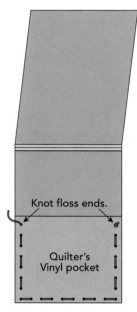

Stitch through Quilter's Vinyl.

Thread Grid

1. The holes made for the Quilter's Vinyl are on the bottom of pages 1, 3, 5, 7, and 9. These same holes are on the top of the even-numbered pages. Thread 6 strands of a different color floss through an embroidery needle, and knot the end. Starting at one of the holes ½˝ from the top edge of an even-numbered page, point the needle down to go through the page and then through the Quilter's Vinyl. Pull the needle all the way through and bring the needle up through the next hole.

2. Pull the needle all the way through, then bring it down through the hole that is diagonally across the page. Bring the needle back up through the hole that is ½˝ below the previous hole. Continue diagonally crossing the page until the last hole. Pull the floss tight and loop it around the floss that is already there. Knot the end, trim, and seal with a dab of glue. This creates a grid to tuck things inside.

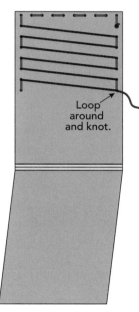

Stitch another grid on even-numbered pages.

Cover Titles and Pocket Titles

1. Using a computer, type your preferred titles in the desired font and color. We used:

Front cover: 4 ME (For Me)

Back cover: TTFN (Ta-Ta For Now)

5 pockets:
BFF (Best Friends Forever)
OMG (Oh My God)
I<3U (I Love You)
TGIF (Thank God It's Friday)
MTE (My Thoughts Exactly)

2. Add a thick outside border to each title and fill in the text box with a contrasting color. Sizes and shapes should match the selected adhesive acrylic dots. Print the titles on paper.

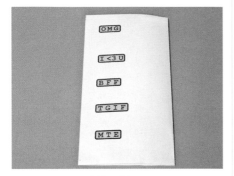
Print titles.

3. Peel adhesive acrylic dots from the liner (hold the stickers by the edge so no fingerprints show on the sticky side) and place one on each title, just a hair inside the border.

4. Trim to size, flush with the edges of the adhesive acrylic dots.

5. To attach the titles to the Quilter's Vinyl pockets, place 2 glue dots on the inside of each end of the acrylic dot and place the title on the pocket, centered near the top edge.

Place titles on pockets.

Front Cover Title

1. Center the metal tag holder near the bottom edge of the book cover; mark holes and punch.

2. Position the title to fit evenly inside the tag holder and adhere it to the fabric with glue dots.

3. Attach the tag holder with 2 brads on top of the title. (Cover the brad stems on the inside with a photo.)

4. Glue seed beads around the edges of the tag holder.

Tag holder and seed beads

Back Cover Title

1. Center the metal tag holder where the spine BatiKit fabric meets the cover batik fabric. Mark holes and punch, being careful to avoid the embroidery floss grid on the inside of the back cover. (If the throat of the puncher is not deep enough, use a craft blade to slice a tiny **X**.)

2. Position the title to fit evenly inside the tag holder and adhere it to the fabric with glue dots.

3. Attach the tag holder with 2 brads at the top of the title. (Cover the brad stems on the inside with items tucked inside the grid.)

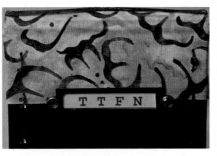
Tag holder on back cover

Picture Inside Cover

1. Center and adhere the 4″ × 6″ cardstock to the inside front cover with glue dots so it fits inside the fabric edges on the sides and the embroidery floss on the top and bottom.

2. Trim and adhere a photo to the cardstock, leaving a ¼″–½″ cardstock border showing. Adhere rickrack or ribbon with glue or glue dots around the photo edge.

3. Adhere rickrack or ribbon with glue or glue dots to the outside front cover over the line where the BatiKit meets the fabric. Glue seed beads on top of the ribbon or rickrack.

4. Cut a 16″–18″ piece of ribbon. Insert it inside one of the center page spreads, wrap it around the spine, and tie a bow.

The finishing touch

I dream
of an Africa
that is at peace
with itself

THESE NO-SEW PROJECTS WILL
FIRE UP YOUR CREATIVE JUICES.

cool projects

Friendship Tin

By Trish Hansen

MATERIALS

- ½ sheet, 6″ x 6″, Princess Mirah's Crafts BatiKit fabric with adhesive backing. See Resources on page 63.

- Rectangular CD tin

- 3–5 assorted coordinating ribbons (approximately 6″ sections)

- Charms and embellishments as desired

- Rotary paper trimmer

- Craft knife

- Ruler

- Cutting mat

Note: For best results, use the recommended cutting tools; however, scissors may be substituted.

INSTRUCTIONS

1. Set the bottom section of the tin aside. Measure the tin top width and length (at the center, not corner to corner).

2. Mark the measurements on the BatiKit and cut out the shape of the lid—**do not** round the corners.

○ Cutting BatiKit

When cutting BatiKit, you've got choices! Use the ruler on your rotary paper trimmer. If you are using velvety BatiKit, cut with the plush side up. A rotary cutter and acrylic ruler on a cutting mat, traditionally used for quilt piecing, cuts great, also. Old-fashioned scissors work every time too, because BatiKit has grid lines on the back for straight, accurate, and easy cutting!

3. Without removing the adhesive, place your cut piece of BatiKit right side up on the work surface. Arrange the ribbons and embellishments. Cut ribbons to length (add 1″ to tuck under the edges of the BatiKit), but **do not** adhere.

● Feeling Sketchy?
A quick sketch or a digital photo can assist you with final placement.

4. Mark the ribbon placement at all points where the ribbon will fold under the BatiKit (mark both the top and bottom of the sheet for best results). Set the embellishments aside.

5. Remove the backing from one corner of the BatiKit, and fold back to expose about 1½″–2″ of the corner.

6. Line up the outside edges of the BatiKit with the edges of the tin top. Tack the BatiKit down at the exposed corner. Check to be sure that all the edges are straight, then gradually peel off the backing.

7. Place ribbon at the ribbon marks, and wrap ½″ ends of ribbon onto the exposed adhesive side of the BatiKit. If you are adding ribbon slides, beads, or other embellishments that will surround the ribbon, be sure to place them before securing the ribbon ends. Smooth the BatiKit into place.

8. Flip the tin top over on the cutting mat so that the fabric side is face down. Trim around the corners using your craft knife.

9. Place any additional embellishments on the tin cover as desired.

Keepsake Box

By Nicole LaCouer
Size: 2¼″ square × 5″ high

- Polymer clay
- Colorfast powdered pigment (copper)
- 12″ of ½″-wide beaded ribbon trim
- Watercolor paints
- Watercolor paper: 3 pieces, 1½″ × 2¾″ each
- Small teal and yellow glass beads
- Glass-finish dimensional adhesive
- Clear acrylic block
- Aluminum foil
- Clear-drying craft glue
- Glue stick
- Double-sided craft tape
- Bone folder
- Black ultra-fine-point permanent marker
- Sewing needle and thread

■■■■■ MATERIALS

For additional product information, see Resources on page 63.

- 2 sheets, 12″ × 12″ each, Princess Mirah's Crafts BatiKit fabric with adhesive backing in coordinating patterns
- 12″ Mirah Crafts ½″-wide rayon ribbon yarn in a complimentary color
- 1/16″-thick chipboard:
  - 4 pieces, 2¼″ × 5″ each
  - 1 piece, 1″ × 5″

- Cardstock (We used tan for the drawers and brown for the lid and embellishments.)
  - 4 pieces, 6″ × 6″ each, for drawers
  - 1 piece, 7″ × 7″, for box lid
  - 3 pieces, 1¾″ × 3″ each, for embellishments
- Rubber stamps (We used a butterfly and a diamond/heart combination.)
- Embossing ink
- Black stamp ink

■■■■ INSTRUCTIONS

Make the Box

1. Cut a 12″ × 6½″ piece of BatiKit for the outside of the box. Place it fabric side down. On the paper liner, using a black ultra-fine-point permanent marker, draw a horizontal line ¾″ up from the bottom.

2. Draw a vertical line ⅞″ in from the left side. Measure 1⅟16″ to the right of that line; draw another vertical line. Measure 2⁵/16″ to the right of that line; draw another vertical line. Continue measuring 2⁵/16″ intervals to draw 3 more vertical lines.

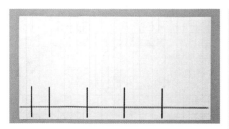

Draw lines on paper side of BatiKit

3. Peel back the BatiKit paper liner from the top edge. Fold and crease on the ¾˝ horizontal line. You will be able to see the vertical lines through the paper. Place the 1˝-wide piece of chipboard first, then the 2¼˝ pieces, from left to right. Align the bottom edge of the chipboard with the creased paper line. Align the left edge of each piece of chipboard with the vertical lines visible through the back of the paper. This will leave ¹⁄₁₆˝ between pieces and ¾˝ around the outer edges.

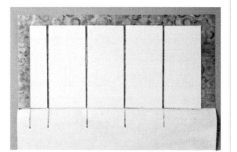

Align chipboard with crease and vertical lines.

● Don't Draw the Lines

Instead of drawing all the vertical lines, draw only the first one on the left. Align the first piece of chipboard with that line, then use a spare piece of chipboard as a spacer between the rest of the panels.

4. Peel the paper liner completely off the BatiKit, trim the corners of the BatiKit (save the triangles that you trim off), and wrap the edges to the inside of the chipboard. Use a bone folder to get sharp creases.

Trim corners before wrapping edges.

5. Stick a BatiKit triangle that was trimmed from the corners (Step 4) over each inside corner edge of the wrapped chipboard.

Triangles finish inside corner edges.

6. To finish the inside of the box, center a 10˝ × 4¾˝ piece of BatiKit over the wrapped chipboard. Center and adhere the BatiKit to the chipboard, smoothing it as you go.

Make the Lid

1. With the 7˝ × 7˝ piece of cardstock, use a pencil and ruler to mark an x from corner to corner. Fold one corner to meet the center of the x, and crease.

2. Bring the folded edge up to the diagonal line, crease, and then open the paper back out. Fold each corner in the same way, opening the paper back out each time. Use a bone folder for crisp creases.

  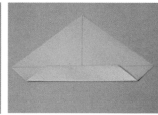

Draw diagonal lines.   **Fold corner to center.**   **Fold again.**

Repeat for all 4 corners.

3. Cut the paper on the part of the 4 fold lines that is marked in red in the photo.

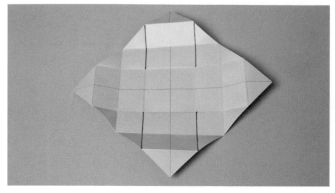

Cut on red lines.

4. Fold the large triangle-shaped "wings" back to the original fold.

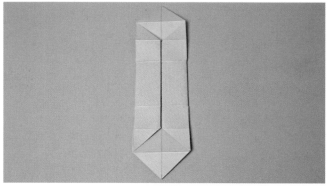

Fold wings back in.

5. Open the folded wings halfway, standing them up to create the sides of the lid. Fold the cut flaps from these wings toward the center, standing them up to create the beginnings of the other 2 sides of the lid.

Sides of lid

6. Fold the remaining flaps up and over the cut flaps from Step 4 to finish forming the sides of the lid.

Fold in remaining flaps.

7. There will be 4 triangles meeting in the center, inside the lid. A little dab of glue or double-sided tape on the inside of the tip will lock these flaps in. Repeat Steps 1–7 using the 6″ × 6″ cardstock to create 4 drawers for inside the box.

Glue or tape down triangle flaps.

Assemble the Box

Place the inside drawer boxes evenly in steps, one on each panel. Start at the bottom and use 1″-wide double-sided craft tape to secure.

Place one box on each panel.

Embellish

1. Stamp a butterfly on the outside of the box on the bottom of each BatiKit panel.

2. Stamp 3 butterfly collages onto the 1½″ × 2¾″ watercolor paper using black stamp ink. Paint with watercolor paints. Once painted, trim close to the stamped image and layer onto brown cardstock, leaving a ⅛″ border. Do this for all 3 painted images. When the paint is dry, apply glass-finish dimensional adhesive. Allow to dry. Glue the images onto the outside of the box in the center of each of the 3 middle panels, ½″ up from the bottom.

3. Cut 2 strips of ribbon yarn, each 5⅛″ long. Stitch beads onto the ribbon in a pleasing array, leaving 1¼″ at one end of the ribbon yarn bead-free. Glue one piece of ribbon yarn vertically along the right edge of the outside of the 1″-wide piece of chipboard. Glue the other piece of ribbon yarn down the center of the last piece of chipboard as shown. This gives a nice finished look to the front of the box. Be sure to place the bead-free end of the ribbon at the top of the box so that the box top will still fit.

Embellish outside of box.

4. Adhere beaded ribbon trim to the bottom edges of the box cover with double-sided craft tape. (Refer to photo at right.)

5. Cover a work surface with tin foil, then roll a small amount of polymer clay into a ball. Flatten it out a bit using a clear acrylic block. Stamp a diamond/ heart design onto the top of the clay. Dust with copper-colored pigment powder. Bake the medallion in the oven according to the clay manufacturer's suggestions.

● Stamping Clay

When stamping into polymer clay, it is a good idea to coat the stamp with ink before you press it into the clay. This will allow for an easy release of the clay.

6. Once the clay medallion is removed from the oven and cooled, apply a generous amount of dimensional adhesive to the piece. This will keep the powder from rubbing off over time, and give a nice shiny finish. While the glaze is still wet, place a wooden bead in the center of the medallion.

7. Cut a 2½″ × 2½″ square of matching BatiKit. Adhere it to the box lid on the diagonal. Glue the medallion in the middle as shown.

Embellish box lid.

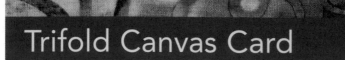

Trifold Canvas Card

By Nicole LaCouer
Size: 4½" × 5¾"

MATERIALS

For additional product information, see Resources on page 63.

- 2 sheets, 12" × 12" each, Princess Mirah's Crafts BatiKit fabric with adhesive backing in coordinating patterns
- 12"–24" Princess Mirah's Crafts ½" wide Batik rayon ribbon yarn in complementary colors
- 4½" × 5¾" trifold canvas pocket
- Rubber stamps: elephant, tiger, giraffe, zebra
- Black stamp ink
- Gold mulberry paper scraps
- 5 pieces, 5" × 7" each cardstock (We used 1 green, 1 black, and 3 cream.)
- 8½" × 11" watercolor paper
- ⅛"-thick dimensional adhesive foam circles or squares
- Iridescent watercolor cakes (We used blue, yellow, green, and gold.)
- 4 misting bottles
- Fibers and ribbons (We used scraps of black, white, and gray.)
- Craft glue
- Alcohol inks (We used rust, creamy yellow, and cranberry.)
- Aluminum foil
- Colored pencils
- Silver permanent marker
- Clear adhesive acrylic drops
- 2½" fern punch
- 1½" × 1½" polymer clay domino

INSTRUCTIONS

Cover

1. Mist all the panels of the trifold canvas pocket with iridescent watercolor paints.

2. Cut BatiKit to 4" × 5⅜". Adhere to the canvas pocket's front cover.

3. Using green cardstock, punch out several fern shapes. Glue these onto the BatiKit on the cover.

4. Stamp 2 elephants onto cream cardstock. Color in the shadow areas of the stamped images with a purple pencil. Trim around the elephant. Trim out the ears from the second stamped elephant. Layer the trimmed ears of the elephant onto the first stamped elephant with dimensional adhesive foam to add dimension. Adhere to the upper left side of the BatiKit on the cover.

5. Cut a contrasting piece of BatiKit, 4" × 1". Glue into place ⅝" up from the bottom of the cover.

6. Print the Nelson Mandela quote *I dream of an Africa that is at peace with itself* onto mulberry paper. Rip around the edges to add a soft feathery feel. Glue onto the cover on the lower right side.

Completed front cover

Interior

1. Cut 3 pieces of BatiKit, 4″ × 3⅛″. Adhere to the top of the pocket panels. Cut 3 matching pieces of BatiKit, 4″ × 1¾″, and adhere to the bottom portions of the canvas pockets.

2. Print out onto watercolor paper the phrases *I dream of an Africa* and *that is at peace with itself*. Layer adhesive acrylic drops directly on top of the words. Trim and mount with glue to the center of the left and right pockets of the canvas.

3. Dip the domino into the various alcohol inks that have been dropped onto aluminum foil. Let it dry. Run the silver permanent marker around the edges of the domino. Stamp *Africa* onto the domino with black permanent ink. Adhere the domino to the middle of the center pocket.

Embellished pocket panels

4. Measure and cut 3 tags 3½″ × 5½″ from black or cream cardstock. Decorate the front of 2 tags with BatiKit and mulberry papers. Tear the edges of the mulberry papers along one edge and layer them on top of the BatiKit to soften the edges. Decorate one tag with a tiger and a black mat border. Decorate the other with a giraffe. Add black, white, and gray fibers around the giraffe.

> **Coordinate Colors**
> *There are several mulberry papers that coordinate beautifully with Princess Mirah's BatiKit fabric.*

5. For the third tag, punch 3 fern shapes from green cardstock. Lay these on top of the tag to use as a mask. Spray watercolor paints in 4 colors onto the tag. Remove the shapes and spray the tag lightly again to soften the look of the mask. Adhere fern punches randomly to the tag as shown. Stamp a zebra onto the tag and emboss.

6. Print onto watercolor paper the words *Peace, Dream,* and *Believe.* Place adhesive acrylic dots directly on top of the words. Trim, and mount 1 word on each tag with craft glue.

7. Finish the tags with fibers and ribbons.

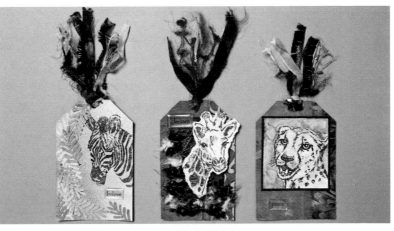

Embellished tags

8. Place the tags in the canvas pockets.

TURN YOUR PATIO INTO AN
EXOTIC PARADISE WITH THESE
SIMPLE, COOL IDEAS AND
VIVIDLY COLORED BATIKS.

the patio scene

Place Mats & Napkins

By Jan Grigsby
Place Mat size: 19½″ × 13½″
Napkin size: 13″ × 13″

MATERIALS

Choose 3 coordinating Princess Mirah Batik fabrics. See Resources on page 63.

- ½ yard Princess Mirah Batik fabric 1*
- ½ yard Princess Mirah Batik fabric 2*
- ⅝ yard Princess Mirah Batik fabric 3*

Enough for 1 place mat and 1 napkin. Choose a napkin style below.

CUTTING

Place Mat

Batik 1

   1 rectangle 18″ × 12″

Batik 2

   1 rectangle, 18″ × 12″

Batik 3

   4 strips 1½″ × width of fabric

Napkin 1 (hemmed edges)

Batik 3

   1 square 14″ × 14″

Napkin 2 (double-sided)

Batik 1 or 2

   1 square 13½″ × 13½″

Batik 3

   1 square 13½″ × 13½″

![icon] INSTRUCTIONS

All seam allowances are ¼".

Place Mat

1. Align a 1½" Batik 3 strip with a long side of the Batik 1 fabric rectangle, right sides together. Stitch together. Trim the Batik 3 strip even with the edge of the rectangle. Press the seam open. Repeat for the other long side of the Batik 1 rectangle.

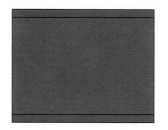

Sew strips to long sides of rectangle.

2. Align a 1½" Batik 3 strip with a short side of the Batik 1 rectangle, right sides together. Stitch together. Trim the Batik 3 strip even with the edge of the rectangle. Press the seam open. Repeat for the other short side of the Batik 1 rectangle.

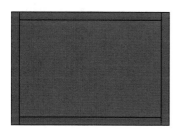

Sew strips to short sides of rectangle.

3. Repeat Steps 1 and 2 with 1½" Batik 3 strips and the Batik 2 rectangle.

4. With right sides together, stitch together the 2 rectangles. Leave an opening for turning. Clip the seam allowance at the corners and turn right side out; press.

5. Press the raw edges at the opening ¼" to the wrong side. Stitch together the opening by hand with a blindstitch.

> ○ **Wow Factor**
> *Instead of stitching the opening with a blindstitch, use a decorative machine stitch. After pressing the opening's raw edges under ¼" to the wrong side, chose a decorative stitch and a complementary thread. Stitch around all 4 place mat sides, ⅛" in from the edge.*

Napkin 1 (hemmed edges)

Press under ¼" to the wrong side on one edge of the 14" × 14" square, turn under another ¼", and press again. Repeat on the remaining sides. This forms the hems that finish the edges. Sew around the square using a straight or decorative stitch, ⅛" in from the edge.

Napkin 2 (double-sided)

1. Place 2 squares, 13½" × 13½", right sides together. Sew together with a ¼" seam allowance, leaving an opening for turning. Clip the seam allowance at the corners, turn right side out, and press.

2. Press the raw edges under ¼" to the wrong side at the opening. Stitch together by hand with a blindstitch.

Mirah Luminaria

By Kiera Lofgreen
Size: 4″ × 6″

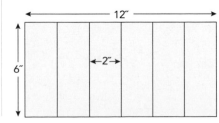

MATERIALS

Instructions will make 2 luminarias.

- 1 sheet, 12″ × 12″, Princess Mirah's Crafts BatiKit fabric with adhesive backing

- Bone folder

- Various punching tools (See Step 4 in Instructions.)

- *Optional: Pinking shears or decorative rotary cutter blade, grommets*

INSTRUCTIONS

1. Cut a sheet of BatiKit in half to make 2 rectangles, each 12″ × 6″.

2. On the lining of each rectangle, draw a light pencil line every 2″ from top to bottom along the 12″ length. This will create 6 equal 2″ × 6″ sections.

```
|←————————— 12″ —————————→|
 _____
|    |    |    |    |    |    |
|    |    |←2″→|    |    |    |
6″   |    |    |    |    |    |
|    |    |    |    |    |    |
|____|____|____|____|____|____|
```

Fold along pencil lines.

3. Fold the BatiKit rectangle, with wrong sides together, along each pencil line. Crease each fold with a bone folder to create 5 sharp creases. (Later, when the 2 short edges are seamed together, you will have a hexagonal cylinder.)

4. Create designs on your cylinder for the candlelight to shine through. You can use paper punches (smaller ones are easier to work with), awls, craft knives, scissors, eyelet setters, and so on. You can also create continuous patterns by running the BatiKit through an unthreaded sewing machine. Experiment with different needles such as twin embroidery or wing tip. If you have access to a machine with fancy stitches, try them out!

> ◉ **Cleaning Your Tools**
> *Be sure to clean your tools after using BatiKit. The adhesive may build up in unexpected places, like the bottom of your sewing machine's presser foot.*

5. Fold the embellished paper in half on the middle line, right sides together. Stitch together the short edges with a scant ⅛″ seam allowance, or staple the edges together with decorative staples.

6. Turn the hexagon right sides out. Iron using low heat, if necessary. Place a tealight in a glass container inside the luminaria, light the candle, and relax!

> ◉ **For More "Punch"**
> *Add metallic grommets as you punch the holes. The candlelight will glint on the metal finish.*
>
> *As a final decorative touch, trim the top edge of the BatiKit cylinder with pinking shears or a decorative rotary cutter blade.*

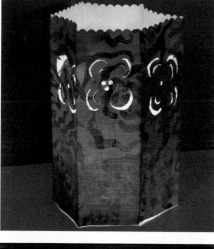

Tray Chic

By Stacy Chamness

MATERIALS

- Princess Mirah's Crafts BatiKit fabric with adhesive backing. See Resources on page 63.

- 1 skein Princess Mirah's Crafts ½"-wide Batik cotton ribbon yarn in a coordinating color

- 1 purchased tray (Ours is bamboo.)

- 4 round wooden balls (2" diameter)

- ½" glass drops

- Fine-point permanent pen

- Scissors and/or craft knife

- Craft or wood glue

- *Optional: Polycrylic protective finish (if you want to waterproof the tray)*

INSTRUCTIONS

1. Choose a design to decorate the tray. If desired, decorate the wooden balls to match. (Later, you will attach them as feet for the tray.)

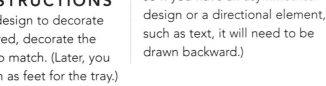

Wooden balls on bottom of tray

> **Less Is More**
> *Simple designs work best.*

2. Analyze your design and decide what parts of the design you want in which BatiKit fabric sheet colors. Use a permanent pen to draw the motif onto the lining side of the BatiKit accordingly. (Bear in mind that the design will be reversed, so if you have an asymmetrical design or a directional element, such as text, it will need to be drawn backward.)

3. Cut out your design from the BatiKit. Position the cutouts on the tray.

4. One cutout at a time, peel the backing off the BatiKit and smooth the piece into place.

5. Cut a piece of ribbon yarn long enough to wrap around a tray handle from edge to edge at least twice. (Lengths will vary; this handle required 18".) Glue one end of the ribbon yarn to the edge of the handle. Carefully wrap the yarn around the handle from the glued edge to the opposite edge and back. Glue the end into place. Repeat for the other handle.

6. Apply glue to the hole side of the wooden balls. Glue the balls onto the bottom of the tray at the 4 corners and let them dry.

7. If desired, apply Polycrylic to the tray face to waterproof it.

Add Decorative Trinkets

1. Trace around a glass drop on the lining side of a BatiKit scrap.

2. Cut out the circle on the inside of the traced line.

3. Peel off the backing and smooth the BatiKit to the flat side of the drop. The drop magnifies the material, creating a beautiful accent for your tray.

4. Glue the glass drop to the edge of the tray. Repeat with as many drops as desired.

> **Magnetic Idea**
> *Create coordinating fridge magnets! Instead of gluing the drop to the tray, simply glue the drop to a magnet.*

> **Make It Easy**
> *A printer or photocopier can be a big help here. Print or copy the design and cut out each element. You can either trace around the cutouts or use the printout as a stencil. Flip the printout over if the element is directional!*

Wine Bottle Hostess Gift

By Theresa Pulido

(If threading the beads is difficult, use a bead threader.) Knot the ends.

3. To make a gift card, brush metallic paint on one side of the cardstock and let dry. Cut a 1¾″ × 3″ piece of BatiKit. Stick it to the painted side of the cardstock, leaving a ¼″ painted border showing on all sides. This is the back of the card.

4. Brush paint on ⅓ of the front of the card and let dry. Cut a 1″ × 2¼″ piece of BatiKit, and stick it to the front of the card, overlapping some of the paint to create a stripe.

5. Punch a hole in the corner of the card. Thread the remaining 16″ length of ribbon yarn through the hole and tie the gift card to the bottle. If you like, thread beads through the ends of this ribbon yarn, as well.

6. Write a note on the plain part of the front of the card.

Personalize your gift card.

MATERIALS

- 2½ yards Princess Mirah's Crafts ¼″-wide Batik cotton ribbon yarn

- 1 wine bottle

- 6–12 medium-sized recycled wood or glass beads

- 2¼″ × 3½″ cardstock

- Iridescent or metallic paint (See Resources, page 63.)

- Scraps of Princess Mirah's Crafts BatiKit fabric with adhesive backing

- *Optional: Bead threader*

INSTRUCTIONS

1. Wrap a yard of the ribbon yarn snugly around the neck of the wine bottle. Tie a knot and clip the ends.

2. Cut 3 strips 16″-long of ribbon yarn. Tie 2 of the 16″ long strips around the neck of the wine bottle, covering the knot. Leave varying lengths of ribbon on each side. Cut the ends of the ribbon yarn at a sharp angle. Twirl each end into a point and thread the ribbon yarn through the beads. Put 3–4 beads on each ribbon yarn end.

Resources

Princess Mirah's Crafts products
Available at www.princessmirah.com

Princess Mirah's Crafts BatiKit fabric sheets with adhesive backing

Princess Mirah's Crafts ½"-wide Batik rayon ribbon yarn

Princess Mirah's Crafts ½" and ¼"-wide Batik cotton ribbon yarn

Princess Mirah's Crafts ½"-wide Batik cotton flannel ribbon yarn

Princess Mirah's Crafts Batik fabric

Princess Mirah's Crafts Batik silk chiffon fabric

Princess Mirah's Crafts Batik silk satin fabric

Boudoir Box, page 25

Beacon Adhesive Gem-Tac glue—www.beaconadhesives.com

Swarovski crystals— www.swarovski.com

Wild Fiber Necklace, page 26

Antico Eyelash Yarn by Trendsetter—color #210*— available at yarn/craft stores

Altered Game Board, page 34

Art Institute Glitter Company Designer Dries Clear Glue— www.artglitter.com

Art Institute Glitter Company Glitter—www.artglitter.com

Weldbond glue— www.weldbondusa.com

La D'ore Leaf and Tape Variegated leafing— www.tolehouse.com/supplies/ papers/goldleaf.htm

Floral Canvas Collage, page 41

Ranger Industries denim color-wash spray   www.rangerink.com

Krylon gold spray webbing and workable fixative—available at craft stores

Create-a-Craft kelly green seed beads—available at craft stores

Pocket Book, page 43

Quilter's Vinyl—www.ctpub.com/ productdetails.cfm?PC=1023

Keepsake Box, page 50

Prickley Pear rubber stamps— www.prickleypear.com

UTEE Ultra Thick embossing ink—available at craft stores

Sculpey Clay—www.sculpey.com

Jacquard Products Pearl Ex (copper)— www.jacquardproducts.com

Trifold Canvas Card, page 54

Prickley Pear tri-fold canvas pocket—www.prickleypear.com

Prickley Pear rubber stamps— www.prickleypear.com

Mr. Ellie Pooh cardstock— store.mrelliepooh.com

LuminArte Twinkling H20's— www.luminarteinc.com

LuminArte Radiant Rain Shimmering Mists— www.luminarteinc.com

Krylon silver marker— available at craft stores

Making Memories Page Pebbles www.makingmemories.com/ products/details/pagepebbles.cfm

Beacon Adhesive Fabri-tac— www.beaconadhesives.com/ cgfab.html

Wine Bottle Hostess Gift, page 62

Jacquard Lumiere paint— www.jacquardproducts.com